COOKING WITH MY SISTERS

HARPER

NEW YORK • LONDON • TORONTO • SYDNEY

Cooking with My Sisters

One Hundred Years of Family Recipes, from Italy to Big Stone Gap

Adriana Trigiani

and Mary Yolanda Trigiani

with Lucia Anna, Antonia, Francesca, and Ida Trigiani

PHOTOGRAPHS BY MARK FERRI
With Antonia Trigiani and additional photographs from the Trigiani family collection, Sally Davies, and Keith Dixon

HarperCollins Books may be purchased for educational, business, or sales promotional use. For information, please email the Special Markets Department at SPsales@harpercollins.com.

Originally published in 2004 by Random House

First Harper Paperbacks edition published 2017.

Designed by Victoria Wong

Library of Congress Cataloging-in-Publication Data has been applied for.

ISBN 978-0-06-246991-5 (pbk.)

17 18 19 20 21   DIX/LSC   10 9 8 7 6 5 4 3 2 1

In loving memory of our divine mom,
and for Anna Christina, Matthew,
Mary Alessandra, Anthony Joseph,
Luca, Ella, and Lucia.
Our traditions are your treasure.

Ida and her grandchildren.

Ida, Francesca, and Toni working in the kitchen.

Ida Bonicelli Trigiani, our mother, at work on her fabulous antipasto.

Contents

Foreword

Welcome to Our Table

*T*here is no better way to feel connected, loved, and complete than to be seated at the kitchen table sharing a meal with those you love.

The recipes in this cookbook—some over one hundred and fifty years old—were handed down through the generations by the women in our family to our mother Ida, and now are shared and served by my sisters, our brothers, and me. As we teach our children, nieces, and nephews these recipes, we're happy to include you in the fun. After all, delicious meals and conversation make life rich and give us a sense that we matter in a world where food is often eaten on the run and the text message seems to have replaced the note in the lunch box.

When we feed our families and friends, we fill them up. We're supporting their good health as our cooking and baking sustains their physical bodies. We are demonstrating a reverence for their souls as we make the connection from our own history and experience to theirs. We're creating a social environment that nurtures them as they share the bounty of your table. It doesn't get any more loving than that. No wonder the Italians made *la tavola* the center of family life—without words, it says who we are. We put effort into a scrumptious meal because you, who are seated there, are worth it.

How lucky I am to be part of that tradition, and to be included, along with my sisters and brothers, in our mother's and grandmothers' kitchens to observe the preparation of daily meals and, on special occasions, traditional dishes honoring holiday celebrations and feast days.

When I look back on my childhood meals, it is with awe, when I remember Mom preparing a family meal every night, with everyone required to be in attendance. It could be said gravy (you might call it sauce) held our family together.

In this updated version of *Cooking with My Sisters*, on the twelfth anniversary of its original publication, much has changed in our lives, but our table, as always, has sustained us. The faces around the table have changed. On August 9, 2017, our mom and cowriter Ida passed peacefully back into the arms of God and her family. We've added two new family members and sent others on to their heavenly reward. There have been moves and changes as life took unexpected turns. But, through it all, we still gather together to share stories and meals at the table, prepared from familiar recipes, reminding us of the women that came before us, who, with skill and delight, fed us and watched us grow.

There is no such thing as excess or too much variety when it comes to meal planning, so I've included some new recipes for your enjoyment. A few of these dishes didn't make the initial cookbook publication for space, and others are new favorites, cherished by my daughter and husband.

If you read cookbooks like novels (as I do), you will find not only sustenance on these pages, but a narrative, in our case, the story of the emigration of four Italian families that shaped our palates and point of view of the world. We come from the Lombardy region in the Alps of northern Italy, the Veneto region, and to the south, Puglia on the cusp of Bari. Our recipes reflect a northern and southern mélange in Italy, and then again in the United States, from small towns in northeastern Pennsylvania and in Minnesota south to Big Stone Gap, Virginia.

The Italian culture is all-inclusive, as every nation and race can lay claim and kinship to being part of the country's history. Surely every family has an appreciation of Italy through the lens of their own experience. We brought our Italian heritage with us wherever we went. Our years in Big Stone Gap had a lasting influence on us. Our gravy was made of tomatoes and served over pasta, while theirs was white and made of flour and pork fat ladled over hot biscuits, but both are called by the same name. Our friends and neighbors in southwest Virginia have grown to love our cuisine as much as we have embraced theirs.

This cookbook represents the world from our kitchen table, and when the meal was fancy, from the dining room table.

It was great fun to revisit family photographs for this new edition. Our mother Ida, the center of our universe, is photographed through the years either preparing a dish, or setting a table, or beautifully dressed next to a table where she lovingly placed every platter, plate, and dish. Every aspect of entertaining was artful to our mother. She set out to make our lives beautiful, and she did it, without fanfare, a big budget, or a panel of experts. She created beauty from her heart. Her mother, Lucia, was dignified and elegant, and so is our mother. Mom cared about the slow and methodical preparation of a meal, but the presentation of that meal was just as important to her. She spent forty years in the Dogwood Garden Club learning the fine points of gardening, landscaping, and arranging flowers. She brought that knowledge into our home and to the table.

The desire to make a good and beautiful life for her children was our mother's definition of what it meant to be Italian. There was the red and white checkered tablecloth on the kitchen table, but there was also the centerpiece of fresh flowers and the candle holder, which she had made herself, out of an old wine flask and layers of colorful wax drippings (melted from our broken crayons!), which she heated and drizzled on to the neck of the bottle, and artfully down the sides in splashes of color. She anchored a taper candle where the cork had been, lit it, and the effect was magical. Her attention to detail made her a good cook and baker and a masterful creator of ambience, where guests were welcome and embraced like family.

That's the feeling I hope you have when you read this cookbook and make these recipes. The past twelve years have brought many gifts, but among the best is you: the enthusiastic reader and your response to this collection. I can't tell you the thrill of seeing you break through a crowd, grateful that we wrote this cookbook, and

Ida and the buffet complete with the candle holder
she made.

I included recipes that you remembered from your own family table, but that had somehow been lost from your family archives, or typical of our grandmothers, had never been written down in the first place.

You are always gleeful at the lost treasure found, so I wanted to make sure that these recipes and our tips would always be available to you. So here they are, with commentary from my sisters, along with some new fabulous recipes, which our family enjoys on a regular basis and hopes that yours will too. There is nothing like a good meal shared at the table with those you love.

May your family enjoy excellent health and happiness in the years ahead with the particular joy that comes from being together sharing a meal lovingly prepared. These moments become memories that become your family story.

Adriana Trigiani
New York City, 2017

Introduction

How We Found the Recipes

M y four sisters and I love to read and we love to entertain. If you're like us, you can curl up as easily with a cookbook as you would the latest hot novel. In these pages we share the family treasure that inspires both passions: the recipes that were handed down to us and the stories that have sustained and enriched us. In our family, food is history and legends are nourishment.

Like many other women of our generation, we learned to cook by watching our mother and our grandmothers. The women of our family, though, tapped the ancient roots of three Italian regions while they adapted their recipes with American innovation and ingredients. From the farm regions of Bari in Puglia to the mountains of Big Stone Gap, Virginia, with winding journeys in between, their legacy reflects the diversity of our Italian experience through a prism of all-American family life.

It takes determination to hang on to old traditions in a new world, and our people had plenty of that. One model of fortitude was Grandmom Yolanda "Viola" Trigiani, our paternal grandmother. She was a direct, bombastic personality (folks used to say, "Here comes the Venetian," when she walked down the street) who became reticent when someone asked for a recipe. She loved secrets and surprises, and both were the fruits of her kitchen.

Grandmom and Adri at a party; Gram borrowed my earrings, fabulous fakes.

The favour of your reply is requested by the thirtieth of November

Dear Adri,
I may need a wheelchair but I'll be there
Love Grandmom.

When we found the recipes, we also found poems and lyrics that Grandmom had written down to read and remember. Here's a sample.

Typical Grandmom. Never one to heap too much salt or guilt, as either could ruin a meal.

After she died, we were cleaning out that kitchen. The oven broke and needed repairs. When my husband pulled it out of the wall, a flurry of small papers flew out from underneath. Caught between the bottom of the oven and the overstuffed drawer just under it were little scraps of paper that floated around like confetti. These scraps bore Grandmom's familiar script. At first, I wondered if Grandmom had been a secret poet like Emily Dickinson, or whether she had stashed love letters from a handsome suitor. No, she had tucked away something of even greater importance: recipes.

I called my sister Lucia Anna immediately to tell her about my discovery, and she was as surprised as I was. (She can be counted on to be precise and methodical; she's a lawyer and had cataloged many of Grandmom's recipes already, thinking we had Viola's complete *oeuvre*.) Not only had Viola hidden recipes in her own kitchen, she even had written some of them in code so they could not be stolen or copied! What kind of clandestine culinary operation was she running, anyway?

Grandmom was no traditional "nonna with the cookie jar." She was a working woman who owned her own blouse mill with her husband. She grew up on a farm, so she knew how to hunt, plant, and pluck. We called her "Granny Get Your Gun" because she was a crack shot with a rifle. (She had an abiding irritation with the groundhogs that populated her lawn, and she let them know it. Right between the eyes. When the 1980s rolled around, we renamed her "Grambo," an homage to fellow Italian Sylvester Stallone of the *Rambo* movies.)

Grandmom's cooking was hearty, and she entertained often. Growing up, we were her assistants in the kitchen. This collection includes recipes Grandmom learned as a young girl, plus notes she took down in her own hand from her in-laws. There are even recipes from friends, scrawled hurriedly on cocktail napkins. In most of them Grandmom wrote down the ingredients but rarely specified the amounts or the techniques of *how* to make them. Whether this was designed to protect her secrets or because she was being creative, or both, I can't be sure. She worked in her kitchen with great gusto and unlimited energy. And since Grandmom loved a party, her cooking took on a special aura when she was preparing a meal for guests. Her enthusiasm and drive were contagious.

When our mother, Ida Bonicelli, met our father, Anthony Trigiani, she discovered that her family was pretty much the opposite of Dad's in every way, including cooking. Mom's mother, Lucia, called Lucy at her request upon her arrival to America, was a gentle soul who never raised her voice. She believed that when there is

Lucy Bonicelli at her kitchen table in Chisholm, Minnesota. She always said, "A navy-and-white dress can go anywhere—it's a classic."

angst at the dinner table, food turns to poison as soon as it's eaten. Grandma Lucy and Grandpa Carlo (we never knew him; he died when Mom was eight years old) were from the Lombardian province of Bergamo. Generally, Alpine Italians are dignified and steadfast in demeanor. This was an apt description of Lucy, in the kitchen and out. She cooked simply yet with great attention to taste; the Bonicelli appetite was smaller but no less oriented to regional traditions and quality values. Cooking was not Lucy's only talent, as she was a renowned seamstress, but as in everything else she did, her attention to detail was eye-catching. I can remember the fresh pasta set out on towels and racks in her spare room, each piece uniform and spaced evenly for drying. Feather-light gnocchi, hearty polenta, and fresh, well-seasoned vegetables were her specialties. Her use of spices and herbs in original ways was the hallmark of her style.

In Lombardy, the dishes were built around starches, lightly buttered or creamed, and roasted meats and vegetables, followed by fruit, when it was available, or light cookies. Grandma Lucy brought this style of cooking with her from Italy, and it shaped the meals prepared in the Bonicelli home when my mom was growing up. This was a significant contrast to the style of my father's family, where Pugliese traditions dominated. Even though she was Venetian, Grandmom Trigiani mastered many southern Italian dishes of the Puglia region, which she learned from her sisters-in-law. They taught her how to prepare pasta dishes in their style—bathed in a marinara sauce and served with pork, sausage, and meatballs. And the main meal had to be followed by elaborate desserts made with heavy cream, sugar, fresh eggs, and butter.

The three regional Italian cuisines and family traditions intersected and merged after my parents married. Meals provided the time to connect after a day of hard work. Nutrition was as much a priority as variety. But there were the battleground dishes, like *braciole*, delicious beef bundles stuffed with basil, butter-soaked bread crumbs, and Parmigiano-Reggiano cheese: Dad liked pine nuts in the filling while Mom preferred none and spritzed fresh lemon on it instead. In this as well as other family standards, they compromised, ending up with inventive twists on authentic Italian recipes.

Bonicelli recipes were precise and clear. Trigiani recipes had to be deciphered or re-created from memory. In this environment, my four sisters, Mary Yolanda ("Mary"), Lucia Anna ("Pia"), Antonia ("Toni"), and Francesca ("Checka"), and I learned to value attention to detail *and* to be cooks who think on our feet. Not to mention territorial about ownership of the various legacies. Recipes and techniques were to be shared among us, but *never* outside the family, until now. *Cooking with My Sisters* brings you into our family kitchen, where the food we prepare is more than the center of our home—it *means* home. Here are our recipes and our stories. *Buon appetito!*

THE BIG LIFE

Perin family, circa 1920s, Delabole Farm, Pennsylvania.

CHAPTER ONE

The Pasta, or as We Called It, Maccheroni

I am the third of seven children: five girls and two boys. Our kitchen was raucous, busy, and the center of our home. To say that we love good food and good conversation—and the occasional knock-down, drag-out "discussion"—is an understatement. It's in our DNA.

No one ever asks what it's like to be a middle child, whether my emotional needs were met in such a large group, or if I had my own room growing up. (The answers: everybody be happy, please; I hope so; and, of course not.) No, the first thing

We tried very hard to be the Partridge Family in the early seventies.

people ask me is, how on earth did your Italian family wind up in the coalfields of southwest Virginia? The short answer is that Dad established a blouse factory there. The long answer is the story we tell in this book.

Our forebears all hailed from hill towns—and mountains, where the work ethic was fueled by hearty peasant food. The dishes we prepare today date back for centuries. And like the recipes that have been handed down for generations from mother to daughter, mother-in-law to daughter-in-law, and grandmother to granddaughter, our family's celebrations are anchored in the familiar stories and legends that are told and retold *a tavola* (at the table). As immigrants from the old country, the Trigianis and the Bonicellis were "vagabond-ohs," as my father used to say proudly. When they left Italy, they packed their native traditions with their needles and thread (making clothes was the family business on both sides) to come to the most exciting country on earth to make their way.

It's no accident that we wound up in the mountains of Virginia. I believe our journey was fated centuries ago, when our ancestors made their decisions in rustic kitchens by old hearths with stews simmering slowly over the fire. We are country people, mountain dwellers. However, in culinary terms it was a leap as wide as the jump from macaroni and sauce to soup beans and cornbread. Making it even more complicated is the dynamic of a large family: Everyone in a big tribe has his or her own view of the events that form the family history.

True to her profession as a librarian, Mom will give you a perfectly honed set of directions. You can imagine the precision of her recipe file. Mom is also a master flower-show judge and a thirty-plus-year veteran of Big Stone Gap's Dogwood Garden Club, which means she can also set a lovely table with a blue-ribbon-quality flower arrangement in the center. Her perfectionism and attention to detail have been gifts to us. She was the first to record many of Grandmom Trigiani's recipes, so we were able to check Viola's Secret Files against Mom's copies.

> ✦ *Mom says:* "Grandma Lucy liked to follow her recipes. Grandmom Trigiani used a recipe only as a guideline or framework. If you watched her make something, it was slightly different every time. And if you asked her how much of something she was putting into a bowl, she would get impatient and ask, 'Why do you need the exact measurements?'"

Mary, my cowriter, likes to improvise from a recipe and be creative in a small dinner-party setting. She never quite got over the fact that six other people entered her space in rapid, noisy progression.

> ✦ *Mary says:* "As the oldest, I'm still searching for peace, quiet, and reason. The chances of finding all are better in the intimate little meal (Bonicelli) versus the rococo extravaganza (Trigiani)."

Pia likes to share family dishes at big dinner parties. She enjoys entertaining and is the queen of warm hospitality.

> ✦ *Pia says:* "I love testing new recipes on my guests, but it's just as much fun for me to prepare the family favorites I've loved for so long."

Toni spent hours in the kitchen with Grandmom Trigiani, and she adores the family traditions. So she has the best perspective on the antics and anecdotes that color our family history. And she is passing these along to our nieces and nephews on their level (at this writing, they're all four years old or under). It's no accident that Toni is their favorite auntie.

✦ *Toni says:* "After the kitchen, my favorite place in the house is wherever the kids are."

Bangor, Pa.
May 12, 1994

Dear Adri:
Congratulations on your engagement. Forgive me. I know that I have no right in the matter, but the prince of Wales wouldn't be good enough for my granddaughters, that is _me_.
I only hope that you do the right thing and if given advice please consider it as everyone is concerned for your happiness.
Please believe me I love you with all my heart and wish you the best.
Love Grandmom.

Viola Trigiani: "But the Prince of Wales wouldn't be good enough for my granddaughters." And we all see what happened with the Prince of Wales. Lesson One: Never let a family member pick out your husband.

From left to right: Grandmom, Pia, Mary, and Mom discuss how to cut the cake. We all remember that the storm blew over quickly.

Francesca, who still answers to her childhood nickname, Checka, has invented brilliant shortcuts for many of our recipes, with delicious results. Like Mom (seven children, one right after the other) before her, Checka (three children, one right after the other, and at this writing, *numero quattro* on the way) has to get the food on the table fast, and it had better be tasty.

> ✦ *Checka says:* "Mom always reminds us that Italians know how to create dishes from whatever they have in their kitchens. It's certainly true in my house!"

And I like to create my own versions of the family favorites, studying the classic recipes, reviewing mine, and then trying something new. I am proud to say that, while I'm a pretty good cook (after all, I was employed at the Mount Bethel Inn in Mount Bethel, Pennsylvania, one fateful summer in the early 1980s), my husband, Tim, learned the keystone dishes from Grandmom Trigiani (once she decided to accept him as my husband and started speaking to him directly).

Grandmom Trigiani taught Mom to make tomato sauce. Now, this would seem a natural thing, mother-in-law to daughter-in-law, both wanting to please the man in the middle. But Grandmom wasn't big on in-laws; she was very clannish, suspicious of anybody "marrying in." Especially if she hadn't hand-selected the person. When Dad wrote to his parents from college and told them that he was going to marry Mom after graduation, Grandmom retained a detective (not a real one, a priest) to contact the Bonicellis' priest in Chisholm, Minnesota, and find out what kind of family Mom came from. When the priest reported back that Mom's people were of sterling character, Viola gave in and accepted the inevitable. (Later, I learned that Grandmom's own father had gone to their family priest to convince Viola *not* to marry a fellow she was seeing. The priest changed Grandmom's mind, which made the way for her to marry Michael A. Trigiani, our grandfather.)

> ✦ *Mom says:* "After Anthony was discharged from the army, after our first year of marriage, we moved to his hometown in Pennsylvania and lived

Our family in Big Stone Gap.

our first year there in his parents' home. Grandmom taught me how to make maccheroni and meatballs (in Italian, *polpette*) the way Anthony liked them; we hadn't eaten pasta that way in my home. This became a standard dish once a week for years to come, and as the family grew, so did the size of the pot."

When we moved to Big Stone Gap and encountered "spaghetti" in the Big Stone Gap Elementary School cafeteria for the first time, it was shocking. The noodles were boiled until you could see through them and then sloshed with sloppy joe mix, heavy on the ground hamburger. We did our best to swing the cafeteria staff toward authentic Eye-talian (as they put it), but we gave up when they insisted that all spaghetti sauce needs is a base of chopped meat, a cup of ketchup, and a shot of chili powder. Our credentials as the only Italians in the school held very little sway.

At home, we made our own pasta several times a year and it was always an event. First, the wooden kitchen table was scrubbed. Second, Mom did an inspection for cleanliness, presence of ingredients, and accuracy of measurements. Finally, Dad put on an apron and would "go ethnic." He did this at every opportunity anyway, like dressing up for Halloween parties (calling himself The Godfather of Poplar Hill, our neighborhood), but he became more Italian with greater gusto when he could toss around some flour. The rest of us got to critique each other's style and rate of production. (Mary hid in her room; she couldn't take the performance pressure.)

The Pasta Making Team consisted of Toni, Checka, and our brother Michael. Occasionally Pia and our brother Carlo would join in, but the core group was pretty solid. Mom observed, mostly as a buffer to Dad, and to make sure that nothing that wasn't in the recipe wound up in the dough.

♦ *Toni says:* "I prepped the kitchen and got the 'tools' for the day ready. Dad was an in-and-out overseer. He would check in at the start of the proceedings and watch the dough being made, and when the cranking started, he always got the first turn to monitor how the dough was working. Once he was satisfied with the proceedings, he would take a nap. When his nap was over, he would come in the kitchen and find the strands of spaghetti drying on the rack. He was as proud of those noodles as he was of a straight-A report card."

Dough for Homemade Pasta (Pasta Fatta in Casa)
SERVES 4 TO 6

8 ounces unbleached, all-purpose flour
1 level teaspoon salt
1 egg
1 tablespoon olive oil
4 tablespoons hot water

Sift the flour and salt onto a large cutting board and make a well in the center. Break the egg into the well and add the oil and water. Using a fork, beat the egg, oil, and water, slowly adding flour from the edges of the crater. Continue to work in all the flour. When it becomes too difficult to use a fork, use your hands to finish mixing.

Flour the board and knead until the dough is fully mixed and does not stick to your fingers. If it sticks, just add a little flour to your hands and keep

Grandpop and his grandchildren at play.

working it in. Make a ball and place in a bowl. Rub olive oil on the dough, cover with plastic wrap, and let sit for at least 15 minutes.

When ready to cut, take a piece from the bowl, knead, and roll out flat.

Now you're ready to make any kind of pasta.

Instructions: Using a machine to make noodle shapes, such as spaghetti, fettucine, and capellini

When using a machine, decide what style pasta you want to make. Sometimes the size of the noodle will determine the thickness of the sheet you need coming out of the roller end. (Sometimes it helps to give a sheet a quick press with the rolling pin before inserting it in the machine.) Once you roll a piece of dough to the desired thickness, you insert the resulting sheet into the farther end of the machine, which makes the uniform strips. You need to have someone cutting the strips horizontally as they come out of the machine, or they'll be a foot long. Lay them flat to dry or hang them on a towel rack to dry. Sprinkle with flour to help the drying and to keep them from sticking together.

Instructions: Making stuffed pasta forms, such as ravioli

When making pasta by hand, you must keep the dough very soft and sticky. We rarely made a small stuffed pasta, and when we did, we used these little ravioli molds that look like ice cube trays. You lay a thin sheet of pasta over the entire mold, "lining" each indentation with the dough, then placing a small bit of filling in each indentation. Then you lay a top sheet of the dough over that and trim away all the excess around each indentation. Then you let them dry for about a day, turning them over so they dry uniformly and don't mold. After that, you can refrigerate or freeze them.

You can always do this without the pasta form by placing "stations" of your filling along a long, narrow sheet of dough, cutting them between each station and sealing them with a serrated pizza cutter.

A Tip from Toni: While you're rolling out one piece of dough, keep the rest covered, preferably in a deep bowl, so that it doesn't dry out. Immediately cut the dough you just flattened into the shape you want and sprinkle with flour. Lay it out to dry so it doesn't stick.

A Tip from Mary: If you're buying pasta, look for those produced from traditional molds. (It will tell you on the package; if it's not there, assume it's modern equipment.) You'll see a real difference—a rougher surface that can grab the sauce and, therefore, more flavor. Plus, they hold their shape longer. I like the Francis Ford Coppola pasta, because he bought the Morisi factory in Brooklyn, where the noodles are still made with the original machines used over a century ago. The pasta has a chewy consistency, which is what makes it *alla rusticana.* If you prefer a lighter, smoother texture, the De Cecco and Barilla pastas are the best.

We didn't start calling maccheroni *pasta* until the 1980s. Even though Mom grew up calling it *pasta asciutta,* we grew up calling it "the macs." Today, we prefer the heartier shapes of southern Italian pastas. They hold the sauce better and are easy to get to the *al dente* state.

Checka or Toni would feed the dough into the machine, and Michael would turn the crank. (Think Charlton Heston in the galley scenes from *Ben Hur*.) Typically, they would repeat this flattening process two more times, adjusting the machine's setting until the pasta reached the desired thickness. (In humid weather, it's more difficult because you have to use more flour.) All the while Michael had to keep the cranking motion constant. When the dough was finally ready to turn into the noodle of choice, they had to adjust the machine to the noodle-making mode. Then Michael or Toni had to be ready to cut the noodles to an appropriate length as the strings came out of the machine.

✦ *Toni says:* "Michael always turned the crank and I fed the dough through, because I knew that flattening the dough and forming the noodles required a gentle, consistent motion, not choppy like Checka's. Michael's technique was always smooth."

When the noodles were cut, we would dry them on a mini towel rack and on clean flour-sack towels in the dining room. At that point, Tiger, our cat, had to be quarantined upstairs, because if you had the towel rack on the floor, the noodles were in swatting range.

Around the time of Tiger's arrival, Dad had detected more infighting than usual among the troops, so in addition to a traditional blessing at the beginning of every meal, he had us all learn the Prayer of Saint Francis, which begins with "Lord make me an instrument of thy peace . . . where there is hatred, let me sow love" and it goes on from there, pretty much covering the territory of good will, kindness, and sacrifice. We said it every night. In this way, Saint Francis, the patron saint of animals, became the patron saint of the Seven Samurai.

When we got Tiger as a kitten, it was in late fall, and she was supposed to sleep outside because Mom just wasn't an animal person. One night, it got really cold, and one by one, we went to Dad to beg him to get Mom to let Tiger sleep inside. Mom was standing her ground. Then Dad asked her, "Ida, what would Saint Francis do?" Mom replied, "Anthony, Saint Francis didn't have seven kids and you to cook and clean for." (Don't worry, Tiger came in from the cold that night and for the remainder of her days. But she *never* climbed up on a table or got near our food.)

Back to The Making of the Pasta. Once the noodles were dry, we used old department-store dress boxes lined with wax paper to store them.

> ✦ *Checka says:* "I always got the job of cleaning the pasta machine—a tedious assignment. This required the use of a paintbrush, per Mom's standards for cleanliness, and always resulted in a final inspection to ensure that the machine was in a pristine state for storage."

Checka maintains that she always got what Dad called scullery jobs because she was the youngest. Not true. All the girls had to deal with the "scullery" moniker and the attendant duties. Which was an endless bone of contention and generated enough *agita* to fuel a union strike. Without fail, if we had company for dinner, Dad would find it amusing to announce that it was time for Scullery to leave the table and wash the dishes by hand. This little routine, generally embellished for guests, got to be particularly irritating after we all moved out, got jobs, and started supporting ourselves.

> ✦ *Checka says:* "When it was Adri's turn to do the dishes, she would begin a discussion about an extremely controversial topic—usually politics. An animated argument would ensue, then end with Adri standing up and making an eloquent statement, often involving tears, followed by a theatrical exit. Pia, Toni, or I—not Mary, because she stood her ground—ended up doing the dishes those nights."

> ✦ *Toni says:* "'Nanny' Julia Isaac, our adopted southern grandmother, finally suggested to Dad that he get Mom an automatic dishwasher. Dad replied, 'What for? I have five right here.'"

Dad eventually gave in to the concept of an automatic dishwasher entering our kitchen (we think he performed the Scullery routine just to get a rise out of us), but the tradition of the women doing the cooking, serving themselves after the men had started eating, and doing all the cleaning prevailed at Grandmom Trigiani's house until she went to her final reward. Grandmom's sister, Aunt Lavinia Spadoni, says she was like this from the get-go. Grandmom was a sexist from day one and had no shame when it came to her belief that men were superior beings whom women were born to serve and obey, at least until you snared one. Of course, you weren't supposed to look at one during your adolescence. But the minute a granddaughter turned eighteen, it was time to start fixing her up with a male of appropriate Italian lineage. Never mind his sexual inclination or habits; if he was Italian and had a pulse, Viola felt he was fair game. A woman could win the Nobel Prize for peace, but she wasn't complete unless she made it to the altar for a full-blown marriage.

We thought the pressure was off after Grandmom passed away, but we were wrong. One of Viola's friends came up to Mary at Dad's memorial service in 2003, six and a half years after Viola's death, and shared the following: "Ooh, your grandmother used to talk about you all the time. She wondered if you'd ever find a husband."

If you were making pasta at Grandmom Trigiani's house, you invariably got snagged into the making of cavatelli, or *chickadays* in the Roseto dialect. (A word about dialect: There are many words for some of these dishes that we have spent years trying to decipher. They sound like Italian words but cannot be found in the Italian dictionary. In this case, Mary thinks *chickaday* came from the verb *ciccare*, which means to boil to the point of anger. Which is what cavatelli do after a few minutes in the hot water.) Cavatelli is a small piece of dough, and the Roseto variation requires an intricate rolling technique that many Trigianis have tried but few have perfected—at least in Viola Trigiani's eyes.

Like the making of noodles with the machine, the making of chickadays required specific people for specific roles. Grandmom rolled the dough through the machine to flatten it, but she kept it thicker for this kind of pasta. (The same flattening could be done with a rolling pin.) Then she would cut the flattened dough into strips. A team of designated "flickers" would be at the ready; they would take a small piece of the dough and roll it back and forth once on the work surface, with the forefinger and middle finger, to create a tiny roll of pasta.

In the beginning, before fingers got tired, we competed to see who could make the most without screwing up. This was not for the weak of heart or those lacking dexterity. If your pieces weren't uniform, both in your own pile or as they compared to other piles, Grandmom went a little vertical and you had to start over. Checka usually lasted the longest because she refrained from complaining, although she was hyper-competitive. She always wanted to see if she could create the largest pile of uniform pieces, and she was willing to sit there for a couple of extra hours to do it.

✦ *Checka says:* "What my sisters have never understood about me is that I did as I was told. If someone wanted me to flick the pasta, I flicked the pasta, and for as long as it would take. I didn't complain—I kept the peace—but of course this has been interpreted as competitive."

Cavatelli (Chickadays)

SERVES 10 TO 12

Use the same ingredients as in the basic dough recipe (see page 9).

From the finished, chilled dough, cut a piece about the size of your fist. On a floured surface, knead and roll until about ¼ inch thick. Cut rolled dough into strips about ½ inch wide and cut into pieces about ¾ inch long.

Working on the same floured surface, place your index and middle fingers on a piece and roll toward yourself until it curls, then flip away from yourself, keeping it hollow in the center. Lightly flour the finished pieces and place in a dry area.

Bring a pot of water to a boil. Add salt to the boiling water. Drop in the pasta and keep stirring, to keep the pieces from sticking together, for about 8 minutes. Remove the pieces with a slotted spoon as they float to the surface, placing in a warm bowl.

Toss with the sauce of your choice and sprinkle with Parmigiano-Reggiano to taste.

Grandmom Trigiani's father, "Nonno" Davide Perin, was from a farming family in the Veneto region. By the time we arrived on the scene, Nonno had snowy white hair, a matching mustache, and twinkling blue eyes. When he came from Italy, he worked hard to buy a beautiful piece of land to farm in the foothills of the Poconos. As children, our dad, his brothers and sister, and the Perin cousins often went to help with the harvesting. It's hard to believe, but in his youth, Nonno Perin worked that farm at night and mined slate in the local quarries by day. To hear Grandmom tell it, they had nothing. Whether or not that was true, they respected their livestock, used every part of an animal, and prided themselves on frugality. They wasted nothing and had undying respect for the value of a dollar.

> ✦ *Pia says:* "Visiting Nonno Perin was like a trip to a different country. In the spring, there were ducklings and chicks pecking around the yard, all fluffy and sweet. Nonno always gave you a big kiss, something awe-inspiring due to the scratchy mustache. He loved to watch us with the animals. One time, he took me into the barn to see a baby bull, who promptly kicked me into a manure pile!"

Dad had a lifelong devotion to good food, and Grandmom had only herself to hold accountable. Dad was the first son. Rumor has it that when he was born, none of his older cousins was allowed to enter the baby's room or touch him. The fact that her first child was a boy was an important accomplishment for Grandmom, who still stung from the comments her parents used to get because she, their first child, was a girl. So Dad got the royal treatment throughout his childhood. By day, when Grandmom was at the blouse factory, Dad stayed with a cousin. This lady made him a fresh *zabaglione*—a sort of an egg custard (see page 146)—every morning, "with an egg plucked fresh from the chicken." On the weekends, the pasta dishes reigned. Sometimes Grandmom made her own jumbo shells or the manicotti tubes, but as she liked to remind us, the most important part was the filling. The ricotta filling our family uses works for the large stuffed shells, manicotti, or homemade ravioli.

When we first moved to Big Stone Gap, Mom had to "import" ricotta from the

Easter on Nonno's farm in Delabole, Pennsylvania. Front row, left to right: Adri, Mary, Toni (bending to pet the dog), and Pia; back row: Nonno, Michael, and Mom.

north. There were a lot of things we couldn't find in southwestern Virginia in the 1970s. You could forget polenta meal, even though corn bread was a staple in the south, and you wouldn't find veal, prosciutto (air-cured Italian ham), fresh Parmigiano-Reggiano cheese, or dried cod (*baccalà*). When Dad came back from a business trip up north with a stash of prosciutto he had a photographic memory of how much he had left in the wrapper before putting it back in the refrigerator. God save the child who had the courage to take a strip without asking first.

Grandmom Trigiani's Ricotta Filling for Stuffed Pastas
MAKES 8 MANICOTTI OR 8 STUFFED SHELLS

1 tablespoon olive oil
2 garlic cloves, minced
2 tablespoons fresh Italian parsley, finely chopped
16 ounces ricotta cheese
2 eggs
½ teaspoon salt
½ teaspoon freshly ground black pepper

Basic Tomato Sauce (page 31)
Grated Parmigiano-Reggiano, for garnish

In a medium skillet, heat the olive oil and add the garlic and parsley; sauté until tender, about 3 minutes.

Pour the garlic and parsley mixture into a large bowl. Add the ricotta, eggs, salt, and pepper and mix well.

Preheat the oven to 375 degrees and grease an 11 × 7-inch baking dish.

Stuff each tube or shell with about ¼ cup of the mixture.

Spread about ½ cup of the tomato sauce on the bottom of the baking dish. Arrange the tubes or shells in a single layer, then cover with another ½ cup (or so) of tomato sauce. Bake until heated through, about 25 minutes. Have grated Parmigiano-Reggiano and a little extra sauce on the table.

> *A Tip from Checka:* Buy the precooked shells and manicotti but focus on making an outstanding filling and sauce. Grandmom always said that's what makes the difference, and she was right. The precooked pasta also reduces the risk of too-chewy or too-soft consistency in the noodle.

Grandmom Trigiani never made a meat filling that we can recall, but Grandma Lucy did.

Grandma Lucy's Meat Filling for Stuffed Pastas
SERVES 8

4 tablespoons (½ stick) unsalted butter
2 garlic cloves, peeled and crushed
2 tablespoons fresh Italian parsley, chopped
2 cups ground beef, veal, or chicken
2 cups plain bread crumbs
½ cup grated Parmigiano-Reggiano
2 eggs, beaten
2 egg yolks
Salt and pepper to taste

In a heavy pan, melt the butter and sauté the garlic and parsley until the garlic is a light brown. Add the meat and cook gently until browned, about 10 minutes. Remove the pan from the heat and let the meat cool. Then add all the other ingredients and mix well. The filling is now ready to add to the pasta form.

For Ravioli

Follow the instructions on page 11 for making stuffed pasta forms.

Bring about 12 cups of water to a rolling boil. Add the pasta, but watch closely; make sure to remove them with a slotted spoon as they bubble to the surface. Transfer directly to a serving dish and cover with the sauce of your choice.

> *A Tip from Checka:* Try boiling these in chicken stock for extra flavor, especially if you prepare these as they do in northern Italy, with just melted butter and Parmigiano-Reggiano—quick, easy, wonderful.

For Manicotti

Preheat the oven to 375 degrees and grease an 11 × 7-inch baking dish.

Stuff each tube or shell with about ¼ cup of the mixture.

Spread about ½ cup of Basic Tomato Sauce (page 31) on the bottom of the baking dish. Arrange the tubes or shells in a single layer, then cover with another ½ cup (or so) of tomato sauce. Bake until heated through, about 25 minutes. Have grated Parmigiano-Reggiano and a little extra sauce on the table.

Grandma Lucy also liked to serve gnocchi, and hers were as light as feathers. This is an excellent alternative to a plain pasta—something different, especially in the winter.

Gnocchi (Dumplings)
SERVES 6

2 pounds floury potatoes, peeled
¼ teaspoon ground nutmeg
1 teaspoon salt
½ teaspoon freshly ground black pepper
2¼ cups unbleached flour
½ cup grated Parmigiano-Reggiano

Boil the potatoes in salted water. Mash them or put them through a ricer into a large bowl. Best to have no lumps.

Add the nutmeg, salt, and pepper. Blend the flour into the mixture, about ⅓ cup at a time. The dough should be smooth.

Divide the dough into about six portions. Roll each portion into a stick or tube, about ¾ inch in diameter.

Cut each stick into 1-inch pieces, on a diagonal. Then, press the tines of a fork into each piece.

Bring 4 quarts of unsalted water to boil. Add the dumplings to the water a few at a time, waiting for them to boil to the surface. When they do, wait about 10 seconds, then, using a slotted spoon, remove them and put them into a warm bowl.

Toss with the sauce of your choosing, or just pats of butter, and sprinkle with Parmigiano-Reggiano to taste.

Grandma Lucy continued to make her own dough and noodles through most of her life, one of the Italian traditions she kept, even as she embraced America and its ways. (She was determined to learn English, so she read several newspapers every day.) Lucy came to America in the early part of the twentieth century with her father, Marco. Work was very scarce in Italy at the time, and at seventeen, Lucy was of an age to work. Their plan was to make enough money to pay for the new family home they were building in Schilpario, then to return there in a couple of years.

Lucy and her father lived in Hoboken, New Jersey, and she worked in a garment factory. Eventually, she was introduced to Carlo Bonicelli, a young man from Vilminore, a neighboring town back home. They had known of each other's families

COOKING WITH MY SISTERS

Carlo Bonicelli, owner of the Progressive Shoe Shop, 5 West Lake Street, Chisholm, Minnesota. Carlo's dream was to design shoes, not just mend them.

in Italy but had never met. They only saw each other a few times over here, but they had begun a written correspondence. When Nonno Marco announced it was time for them to return to Italy, Carlo raced to Marco to ask for Lucy's hand in marriage. They were wed just a few hours before Marco set sail for the return trip to Italy. Lucy never went back, and she never saw her parents or any of her five siblings again, except for her youngest brother, Andrea, who traveled to the states many years later.

Carlo had earned his U.S. citizenship by enlisting to fight in France during World War One. After they married, Carlo and Lucy moved to Chisholm, on northern Minnesota's Iron Range, so that he could get work in the taconite (iron ore) mines there. He soon learned, though, that the miner's life was not for him, so he opened a shoe shop.

✦ *Mom says:* "Papa used to laugh a lot. I remember listening at night while he entertained some of his friends in the shop. They were always laughing, and Papa loved to keep them there late. But he brought Mama her coffee in bed every morning, no matter how late he had been up the night before."

When he got sick and knew that his time was short, Carlo asked Lucy to take their three children—Orlando, Mom, and her twin sister, Irma—back to Italy, where there was family to look after them. She told him she would think about it, although her mind was made up that she would stay in America. Grandma Lucy said later that she couldn't imagine returning to Italy, where she would have to rely on the charity of her family to survive. Widows didn't work outside the home. Instead, they depended on their families to support them. Lucy's biggest fear was becoming a burden, and that would hold true for her entire life. Besides, Lucy liked America and had earned her own citizenship through her marriage to Carlo. So as a young widow at the age of thirty-four, Lucy stayed in Minnesota, learned to read and write English, and supported herself and her children by operating the shoe store Carlo had opened and performing clothing alterations in the back. Her three children went on to become college graduates, a real legacy for an immigrant seamstress. Grandma Lucy never remarried.

Our mother, Ida (bob haircut), with her father and friends in the background, in an undated photograph. Chisholm. 1930s.

CHAPTER TWO

The Sauce

In a large Italian family, cooking signifies bonding or bondage, depending on your point of view and the chores you're assigned. If it's not made to be fun from an early age, or if only the least desirable tasks are delegated to the junior members, the whole experience gets tainted. Fortunately for us, the burdensome aspects of apprenticeship were offset by the satisfaction of working together to create something the entire family could enjoy.

Which brings me to The Canning of the Tomatoes. This happened in Grandmom Trigiani's basement kitchen. Many Italians never throw things away, so instead of getting rid of the old refrigerator and stove, they simply move them into the basement—and *pronto*, the messier jobs can be executed on the old equipment.

Until Grandmom got older, she did her canning solo. She produced so many quarts each year that the jars lined up in her pantry—and the pantries of her four children—were a sight to behold. Viola was a human assembly line, so her expectations for rate and quality of production were unusually, if not unreasonably, high. This meant that you *really* had to want to learn how to can tomatoes. Or you had to be willing to suffer the indignities of elbow jabs and dark looks from Viola just to remain in her favor.

> ✦ *Mary says:* "I simply did not have that great a desire to learn how to can tomatoes."

> ✦ *Toni says:* "This is why Viola's namesake (Mary is, after all, Mary Yolanda) was to miss out on one of the truly challenging rites of passage for a Trigiani female. Poignant, isn't it?"

By the way, in the family, we often call Mary by her full name, sometimes shifting to Mary Viola when we want to get a reaction. The way "Yolanda" became "Viola" is a little immigrant story in and of itself.

Even though Grandmom was born in the United States, her family was ethnically Italian in a part of Pennsylvania that was largely Welsh and German. When the young Yolanda headed to school around 1913 or so, she encountered teachers who had difficulty pronouncing some of the children's names. "Yolanda" and "Viola" have the same Latin root; so one teacher undoubtedly thought she was doing Grandmom a favor by anglicizing her name.

Grandmom Trigiani's parents, Davide and Giuseppina Perin, had given some of their six children—Yolanda, Ines, Vittorio, Elena, Battista, and Lavinia—names from Italy's royal family. (Lavinia's name was inspired by a funeral mass card. Ap-

Grandpop with Pia, and Grandmom holding Mary, at Pia's birthday bash.

propriate, because Lavinia was George Bernard Shaw's Roman martyr.) We don't know if this is a coincidence or if our great-grandparents had these names in their families as well. In parts of Italy, the tradition is to name the first son and the first daughter for the father's parents, the second son and the second daughter for the mother's parents. Grandmom and Grandpop Trigiani followed this tradition, and so did our parents.

Dad's paternal grandfather, Antonio, was, by all accounts, a colorful character. Dad used to tell us that Antonio was AWOL from the Italian army when he stowed away on a ship to America. Antonio was, however, legal on this side of the Atlantic and took great pride in serving as custodian of the Roseto elementary school, named the Columbus School, for that Italian icon. Antonio was a janitor who had the job of ringing the bell and raising the American flag, and while we never knew him, we knew that our grandfather and his brothers and sisters grew up with great respect and affection for this country. Grandpop Michael Trigiani, Antonio's son and Dad's father, eventually served as chief burgess (mayor) of Roseto.

Back to The Canning of the Tomatoes, which Toni found so over-the-top that she videotaped it.

> ✦ *Toni says:* "The best was the year Pia picked up the tomatoes on her way to Grandmom's. She asked Pia how much she had paid for the bushel, and Pia, not thinking fast enough to cut the number in half, actually gave Grandmom the true figure. Grandmom lost it."

> ✦ *Pia says:* "As I recall, I did fudge the numbers, but it was still too high for Grandmom."

> ✦ *Checka says:* "The whole thing made Canning 101 highly entertaining."

The finished product—vivid and eye-catching even in a basic Mason jar—was prized by anyone lucky enough to be the recipient of Grandmom Trigiani's largesse. For all our childhoods, the basic tomato sauce was always made with at least one pint of Grandmom's canned tomatoes at the bottom of the largest saucepot in the house. If you visit our kitchens today, seven years after Grandmom's death, you'll find a jar or two of her tomatoes. Now, though, it's a precious heirloom, never to be opened but to remind us of our roots.

Basic Tomato Sauce
MAKES ENOUGH FOR 12 SERVINGS OF PASTA

2 quarts (64 ounces) tomatoes, puréed
Two 6-ounce cans of tomato paste
Five 6-ounce cans of water (use the cans of tomato paste to measure)
2 teaspoons garlic salt
2 teaspoons freshly ground black pepper
2 tablespoons olive oil
2 tablespoons Italian seasoning (available premixed)
One 4- to 6-ounce pork bone with meat still on it
½ teaspoon salt

Combine the tomato purée, tomato paste, and water in a large pot and simmer over very low heat. Add the garlic salt, pepper, and 1 tablespoon of the olive oil. Stir well, ensuring that the tomato paste is blending completely. Sprinkle the Italian seasoning in a thin layer on the top.

Sauté the pork bone separately in a little of the olive oil and the salt. Cook fully, then add to the sauce. Stir again, allowing the Italian seasoning to blend.

Let the sauce simmer, covered, for 3 to 4 hours over very, very low heat.

> *A Tip from Mary:* If you're not using your own, the best canned tomatoes to buy are the San Marzano variety, imported from Italy. Italian specialty groceries usually have them. There are a few brands, all offering excellent quality.

The secret of our sauce is to let it cook its way to a depth of flavor possible only with meatballs simmering in the pot. If you can make some time to prepare our basic sauce ahead of time, even freezing it, it's amazing how you can turn a weekday meal into the real Italian thing.

You can get the sauce started in a large pot while you make the meatballs. Grandmom liked to sauté her meatballs before placing them in the pot; Mom just put them right in without the frying.

Meatballs
MAKES 36 PIECES, SERVING 12

3 ½ *pounds coarsely ground lean beef* *
2 *cups Seasoned Bread Crumbs (page 34)*
½ *cup chopped fresh Italian parsley (or 4 tablespoons dried parsley flakes)*
½ *cup grated Parmigiano-Reggiano*
5 *eggs*

---

* You can alter the recipe by using a mixture of ground veal, ground beef, and/or ground sausage. We always use very lean plain ground beef.

1½ *cups whole milk*
1½ *teaspoons freshly ground black pepper*
½ *tablespoon garlic salt*

Add all ingredients in a bowl and mix well. If the mixture is too soft, add more bread crumbs. Make balls about 3 inches in diameter, firm but not hard. Wet your hands and roll one more time. Drop in simmering sauce.

> *A Tip from Pia:* Use the leanest meat you can find—and ground beef is just fine. If you like veal, great, but we always used plain old ground beef.

> *A Tip from Toni:* Try using your hands—squeaky clean, of course—to do the first mixing of ingredients in the bowl. It's the most efficient way, and it's easier to tell if the mixture is too soft.

Seasoned Bread Crumbs

3 *stalks of Italian parsley, stems removed and leaves chopped*
1 *teaspoon salt*
3 *stalks of fresh basil, stems removed and leaves chopped*
¼ *cup olive oil*
1 *loaf of Italian bread, broken into pieces*

Preheat the oven to the lowest temperature possible.

In a small bowl, combine all the ingredients except the bread.

Place the bread in a large bowl and pour the mixture over it. Toss.

Place the coated pieces on a cookie sheet, and bake for 1½ hours. Remove and let cool.

Crumble the pieces for use in a salad. Use a hand grater or food processor to make fine crumbs for use in recipes.

Grandpop Trigiani was as gentle as Grandmom was forceful. Visitors to their household always marveled at his patience, as Grandmom was definitely a handful. Lucky for our mother, Ida, he was in the picture when she married Dad. Having lost her own father at a young age, one of the benefits of her marriage to Dad was her time with Grandpop. And since Dad had a temperament similar to Grandmom's, Mom and Grandpop often ended up in cahoots together. Mom worshipped Grandpop, and his sister, Aunt Mary Farino, told her that the feeling was mutual. Grandpop had told Aunt Mary, "There are daughters-in-law and daughters-in-law, but there's only one Ida." Aunt Mary became an important influence on my work. She taught me about old movies, introducing me to the films of Bette Davis, Myrna Loy, Clark Gable, and Spencer Tracy. Aunt Mary saved copies of *Photoplay* and *Modern Screen* from the 1930s and '40s, which I treasured years later.

Before I arrived on the scene, Mom, Dad, Mary, and Pia moved from our grandparents' home to a flat nearby, in an old funeral home that Mom and Dad converted to apartments. As long as we lived there, Grandpop used to come to make wine in the basement. He told Mom that the temperature and humidity down there were perfect for making wine, so he used to arrive in September with crates of purple grapes. When he was finished squeezing the juice from the grapes, he would spread the skins around Mom's flower beds. The backyard would have the aroma of the grapes for weeks afterward.

✦ *Mary says:* "To this day, when I visit wineries in the Napa Valley, the smells of the barrel rooms always remind me of Grandpop."

✦ *Pia says:* "Grandpop was quite a character—fun-loving and devilish yet sweet. He got his start in the blouse mill as a machinist, and he always puttered around his garage, fixing things. And, he loved to take pictures and make films. Grandpop was creative with a movie camera. He actually built a rig on his car to film a tracking shot of a crowd of people after a wedding!"

Our family wears our Sunday best.

Grandpop called me Rebel, for Rebel Yell, the whiskey he discovered after we moved down south. He taught me three fundamentals: how to eat soup properly, how to tie my shoes, and how to play checkers. Like his wife, he would reuse things rather than throw them away, so if a batch of his wine turned, he would bottle it as wine vinegar. (As kids, we always wondered why the vinegar we bought in the store was clear and didn't have sediment at the bottom of the bottle.)

We lost Grandpop before we were old enough to be of any help to him down in the basement. The older ones of us do remember, though, how much he loved his grandchildren and took delight in teaching them to swim (by throwing them into the pool and yelling, "Swim! Swim!"), giving them rides on his tractor and golf cart (purchased after a stroke to help him get around), and enlisting them to tease Grandmom.

You had to drag the family stories out of Grandmom Trigiani, and they were generally darker than the reality. Having moved to Big Stone Gap, we craved the legends. Cooking with Grandmom was one way to get closer to the roots we pulled up when we moved to Virginia. On the other hand, Dad was the storyteller. The process of the cooking and eating was his stage. It was probably over a meal that we learned about his Great-Grandpop Antonio and the AWOL/stowaway legend. Dad genuinely liked his relatives and their tales, no matter how outlandish.

In many ways, Dad never left Pennsylvania, even though by his death in 2002 he had spent a third of his life in Big Stone Gap. There were things he enjoyed about Virginia very much: sausage biscuits, mountain music on Saturday nights at the Carter Family Fold, and covered-dish suppers at church. Still, his attachment to Roseto ran deep, and he kept the traditions he learned there. Dad remained a Rosetan to the end.

♦ *Mary says:* "I'm still not over that leave-taking from Pennsylvania. I was nine years old. It was so difficult to say good-bye to Grandpop, especially. But the move to Big Stone Gap turned out to be good for all of us."

♦ *Toni says:* "As little kids, we didn't really understand what was going on and we missed the family. But now I think that we actually wound up working harder at maintaining our traditions. And, we learned tolerance early on because we really had minority status in Big Stone Gap."

I was excited to be moving to a big house with stairs, wherever it was. I loved our flat in Pennsylvania with its low modern furniture, but the house in Big Stone Gap was completely different—old and huge like a haunted house in a storybook. Besides having to get us ready for a new school, Mom would have to get the house into a more current condition. It hadn't been occupied for years.

♦ *Mom says:* "For the first few weeks, the children were running around with noses black from coal dust as I scrubbed the woodwork and walls. It was such a job!"

Underneath all the grime was some of the most beautiful hand-carved woodwork you would ever see. It was Mom's first house, too, and to this day it's her oasis.

For us, the big challenge would be negotiating the seismic shift from Our Lady of Mount Carmel (run by the Italian order of Salesian Sisters, whose motto was "Mary, Help of Christians, Pray for Us") in Roseto, which was still 99.9 percent Italian, to the Big Stone Gap Elementary School (Scots-Irish predominantly, still bearing a well-deserved grudge from the Stuart years in merry old England). No nuns, no uniforms—but on the plus side, a cafeteria.

✦ *Pia says:* "Going to school for the first time in Big Stone Gap was a trip. It was just the four oldest girls, in matching dresses and head scarves. We must have looked like we landed from another planet. The school buildings were from the early part of the century, and the hardwood floors were kept oiled. Then, there was recess—a new concept for us parochial-school veterans. But the biggest shock were the snack machines, complete with grape soda and Pepsi and peanuts. We learned that first week how to pour the peanuts into a soft drink and eat/drink them that way. Mom registered severe culture shock upon hearing about it."

The old kitchen of the big house produced a lot of great meals and is the center of many of our favorite family stories, not just the wellspring of my fictional tales. Probably one of the first meals Mom made there was spaghetti and meatballs. When there was time or we hosted a larger or more special gathering, she would add braciole (page 61) and fresh sausage (if Dad brought some home from up north).

Of course, there was always *shway-shway* (we're not sure where this dialect phrase originates), a quick version of tomato sauce that many Roseto men perfected as a shortcut. Dad wrote this down for us years ago and even had Mom type it.

Quick Tomato Sauce (Shway-Shway)
SERVES 6

5 tablespoons olive oil
½ medium onion, diced
4 garlic cloves, minced

1 tablespoon capers

1 quart home-canned tomatoes or one 28-ounce can peeled tomatoes, quartered

½ teaspoon chopped fresh oregano

½ teaspoon chopped fresh basil

½ teaspoon freshly ground black pepper

½ cup Zinfandel or Chianti wine

½ cup grated Parmigiano-Reggiano

Pour the olive oil into a large skillet, add the onion, garlic, and capers, and stir to coat the vegetables. Cook over low heat, stirring, for about 5 minutes, until the vegetables are translucent.

Pour the tomatoes into the skillet, crushing and mashing them as they heat. Add the oregano, basil, and pepper. Stir occasionally but let simmer for 15 minutes over medium heat.

Prepare the pasta of your choice. Two minutes before the pasta has finished cooking, add the wine to the sauce and lower the heat to almost nothing.

Easter in Big Stone Gap: the swinging seventies. Front row, from left: Michael, Carlo, Francesca. Back row, from left: Toni, Mary (in her hose that came out of an egg), Pia (head down), and Adri.

"Hope you are all behaving for everybody's sake." Viola Trigiani

Dear Adri,
Just saw this in the paper so I decided to send it to you. How's everything? Hope you are all behaving for everybody sake.
Love Grandmom.

Pour the sauce over the pasta and toss with grated Parmigiano-Reggiano. Serve.

> 🦪 *A Tip from Adri:* Never rinse pasta after boiling, under any circumstances. The noodles will hold the flavor of the sauce better.

Mom always served the spaghetti (or rigatoni, if we begged, but Mom liked to stick to spaghetti) and meatballs with a fresh salad. And we didn't eat bread with it, mainly because you couldn't get Italian bread in Big Stone Gap at that time. Sometimes Mom and Dad would have a small glass of red wine. We kids couldn't have anything to drink until after we ate. We're not sure that Dr. Spock or Dr. Brazelton would approve, but Mom and Dad concluded that we couldn't clean our plates if we were taking in a lot of fluid during the meal. So they declared a moratorium on beverages while we were eating.

✦ *Toni says:* "The No Drinking During Dinner Ban went into effect when Checka started eating grown-up food and refused to eat anything green. Dad figured that if she wasn't drinking, she'd be hungrier and would eat more. Instead, Checka became adept at pushing the greens around her plate, and because she was the youngest, got away with it. Checka still avoids green vegetables, but she has been known to throw back some wine during dinner."

For parties and special occasions we'd veer away from the basic marinara sauce and do something different, like an *arrabbiata* sauce. This spicy version of the basic marinara sauce can add a lot of interest to pasta. (*Arrabbiata* means angry in the case of a person, and in the case of a dog, mad.) We think that Dad liked to make the arrabbiata sauce just so he could ask Checka if she was arrabbiata. Of course, it's now Checka who wears the mantle of best arrabbiata sauce maker in the clan.

✦ *Checka says:* "If I was arrabbiata, it was usually for a good reason. And, I'd like to add that I have no idea what Toni is talking about regarding my wine consumption."

Arrabbiata Sauce

SERVES 4 TO 6 (USING 1 POUND OF PENNE PASTA)

2 tablespoons olive oil
3 tablespoons minced garlic
½ small onion, minced
1 small hot pepper, seeded and finely chopped
2 cups Basic Tomato Sauce (page 31)
¼ teaspoon salt
½ teaspoon freshly ground black pepper
3 tablespoons chopped Italian parsley
½ cup grated Parmigiano-Reggiano

Heat the olive oil in a saucepan. Add the garlic, onion, and hot pepper and sauté for about 1 minute, stirring constantly. Add the tomato sauce, salt, and black pepper. Cook on low heat for about 10 minutes. When it begins to bubble, it's ready to combine with the pasta.

Toss the sauce over the pasta with the parsley. Serve the Parmigiano tableside.

A Tip from Checka: Be sure to wear kitchen gloves when you're seeding and preparing the hot pepper. And don't touch your eyes!

A Tip from Mary: Try adding chopped black olives—very interesting.

COOKING WITH MY SISTERS

Checka's Alternate Recipe for a Quick Arrabbiata Sauce

½ small onion, minced
2 tablespoons olive oil
2 cups Basic Tomato Sauce (page 31)
Prepared hot sauce to taste
3 tablespoons Italian seasoning

Cook the onion in the olive oil until it is translucent. Add the tomato sauce and hot sauce (the amount depends on how hot you want it). Coat the top of the sauce with Italian seasoning and cook over low heat. When the sauce begins to bubble, it is ready to add to your pasta (penne is preferable since it will hold the sauce nicely).

The arrabbiata sauce came onto the scene later, after the older kids had left for college, and still later came the white sauces that our brothers perfected. (We don't include those here because we never really ate them growing up.) But another sauce that Grandmom Trigiani liked to make was her Tuna and Tomato Sauce, a variation that embellishes the *shway-shway* sauce. She generally made this on Fridays during Lent.

Grandmom Trigiani's Tuna and Tomato (Tonno e Pomodoro) Sauce
SERVES 8

4 tablespoons olive oil
12 to 13 ounces albacore tuna (look for Italian brands, packed in olive oil)
7 cups crushed tomatoes (two 28-ounce cans)
6 sprigs of fresh Italian parsley, finely chopped
2 teaspoons chopped fresh basil
Salt and freshly ground black pepper to taste
2 pounds pasta, cooked

Heat the oil in a large saucepan over medium heat. Add the tuna, including the oil in which it was packed, and stir until it's just heated through. Add the toma-

toes, parsley, basil, salt, and pepper. Bring to a boil and then reduce immediately to a simmer. Cook uncovered for about 45 minutes. Toss with the pasta and serve immediately.

Another sauce we liked to make, particularly when we had company coming, was a warm olive oil and garlic dressing. It's especially good on freshly made pasta and more delicate noodles like spaghettini or capellini. Grandpop Trigiani loved to toss pasta with oil and garlic. This was also perfect for a quick lunch, with some cold chicken or pork chops on the side.

Oil and Garlic Sauce
SERVES 8

6 tablespoons olive oil
12 garlic cloves, minced
1 cup chicken broth, fat removed
2 teaspoons grated lemon zest
6 tablespoons fresh lemon juice
6 tablespoons chopped onion
2 teaspoons chopped Italian parsley
2 teaspoons salt
½ teaspoon freshly ground black pepper
5 tablespoons grated Parmigiano-Reggiano

Heat the oil in a large skillet over low heat. When it's hot, add the garlic and cook for about 5 minutes. Add the broth, lemon zest, lemon juice, onion, parsley, salt, and pepper and cook for about a minute.

Toss over the pasta and sprinkle with the Parmigiano. Serve.

A *Tip from Pia:* If you're having a large buffet-style dinner party, or even a cocktail party, you can still serve pasta—just avoid the long versions that are difficult to eat.

Grandmom Trigiani's veal sauce made use of a succulent slow-cooked veal roast and its broth. The sauce was perfect for the evenings you wanted to serve something elegant and spend time with guests outside of the kitchen.

Grandmom Trigiani's Veal Sauce

SERVES 6

One 2-pound veal roast with bone in
3 large onions, sliced
⅓ cup chopped Italian parsley
3 tablespoons flour
2 quarts water
Salt and freshly ground black pepper to taste

In a deep saucepot, brown the veal well. Add the onions and parsley on top, cover, and cook for 1 hour. Remove the meat to a plate. Add the flour and water to the pot and stir to thicken. Season with salt and pepper. Return the meat to the pot and cook for an additional hour.

The Bonicellis followed the more traditional style of dining: In Italy, pasta is served after a light savory course (*antipasto*) and before a *secondo piatto* (second course) of meat and vegetables, then the *insalata* (salad). The Trigianis, on the other hand, made pasta the center of the meal, which is why we think Grandmom's tomato sauce became the basis of our family's cooking traditions. Yet under Mom's guidance, our pasta dinners came to represent the best in the blending of our forebears' regions: spicy, upfront, warm, and generous.

Left to right: Aunt Tiny, cousin Rip and Kitty, Dad and Aunt Lavinia.

THE BIG DISH

Sonny.

CHAPTER THREE

Family Dinners

Grandmom's dining room.

rowing up, it often seemed that just as we were finishing one meal we were preparing for the next. Cooking for such a large family almost made the day-to-day process a marathon. To keep it as efficient as possible, Mom made things simply. We did not eat Italian food every evening, but the way we ate was definitely *all'italiana*, or Italian style: always seasoned, always balanced, always hearty, and more than enough to go around. *Abbondanza!*

One of Mom's basic rules for managing the marathon was keeping the dinner hour, and our participation in it, immutable. We were rarely excused from dinner to attend an event, whether it was academic, sports, theater, or music. (And a kid could walk from one end of Big Stone Gap to the other, so there was no excuse to be late.) Dinner started when it was time to call Dad to the table, usually in the vicinity of six P.M.

Another advantage of having a standard dinner hour was the guaranteed daily opportunity for Dad to reinforce our values, especially a respect for family and cultural traditions. The Big Stone Gap environment was about as non-Italian as you could get, so sustaining *la moda italiana* was an ongoing challenge. For those of us who remembered Pennsylvania, it was as if we had left the earth we knew.

> ✦ *Mary says:* "I swear that I did not know we were Italian until we
> moved to Virginia."

Our entire world had been populated by people who had names like ours and who looked like us. (And not because we were all related, either!) Dad's effort to keep us attached to his family's tradition was deliberate and up-front. Even our phone calls with friends provided a lab for Italianizing. If he detected any hint of a phony southern drawl, he would remind us that the way people talked in our new town was beautiful, but it wasn't us.

> ✦ *Toni says:* "Adri had the Virginia drawl down pat. She could turn it on
> and off just like a faucet."

In Big Stone Gap, the closest thing we had to Italy was Italy Bottom, where the few Italian immigrant coal miners had once lived. Most of them had gone back to the old country as soon as they saved up enough to return. If they had left any descendants, their names had been anglicized. All of this just encouraged Dad to tell more stories. One of his favorites was about Great-Grandpop Antonio Trigiani, who had a thing about children singing at the table. In his half-English, half-Pugliese dialect, Dad's grandfather would announce, "*Chi che canta al tavola e piu stupide di quello*

Adri, cousin Michael Godfrey, and Pia sightsee on High Knob.

che fum' a let'," or something like that. Translated: "He who sings at the table is more stupid than the one who smokes in bed."

✦ *Pia says:* "For the record, we never sang at the table or smoked in bed."

For Mom, the dinner hour provided a platform for enforcing rules of etiquette. Family meals were workshops designed to enhance our manners and demeanor. On report card night, while Dad concentrated on the main subjects, Mom focused on what the Big Stone Gap schools called "deportment." If anyone got less than an A, we knew we'd hear from Mom that the easiest subject in which to earn an A was deportment.

The activity around the table wasn't always of an edifying nature, however. For example, Dad loved to turn his eyelids inside out while everyone else was eating. And he enjoyed creating diversions that enabled him to pinch his favorite items from a nearby plate, usually Carlo's or Michael's (they always sat next to him), whereupon Dad would always swear that he was just "testing to make sure it was fit for human consumption." It was years before we understood this meant that he just wanted more dessert.

Mom's sense of propriety even extended to the preparation of baby food. She never fed a child a cold bottle. How she managed this on trips, before microwaves, especially with so many little ones at once, I'll never know. But a warm formula for babies and a balanced diet for adults was the only way.

We were lucky, because if it were up to Dad to outline the menus, we would have had beef or pasta every night, with a fantastic dessert to follow. In fact, we generally supported his choices, and to this day we remain eternally grateful that he declared a moratorium on liver and stuffed cabbage. (You will find neither in this book. He didn't like eggplant, either, so we have yet to develop any eggplant-based recipes.) Besides the salad and a meat or main course, Mom always made sure we had a good vegetable side dish. So while she reduced the multiple-course format of traditional Italian dining, Mom covered the essentials. It's definitely more relaxing, and exotic, to eat over a span of three hours in a leisurely fashion (the way many Italians still do), but we were all-American in the efficiency department. We had to be, with so many people to manage and so much to get done.

Now that we have children of our own, we marvel at how Mom not only produced seven children in nine years, but did it in such an *organized* fashion. The fact that we had a nice dinner every night as kids had a huge influence on our ability to put on a lovely dinner ourselves. And, no surprise, this extends to the setting of the table. We have a running argument among the sisters over who got the job most consistently. Whoever did it, the job description included correct placement of napkin, flatware, and glassware around the plate.

Mom's emphasis on good manners made us receptive to watching and learning from others. It also gave us the basics for entertaining, something our parents did very well. Many of the dishes we grew up eating in the kitchen are now served in our dining rooms for dinner parties. Not because they're fancy but because they taste good.

◆ *Mary says:* "I like to eat out, so I can always go out to a fabu restaurant to eat delicious food styled beautifully on the plate. When I'm making dinner, I like to focus on preparing meals that I can cook with friends and that will look great without being pretentious."

◆ *Checka says:* "Yeah, but Mary puts a lot of weird stuff in her dishes— like mandarin oranges in turkey stuffing and peas in tuna casserole. P.U."

Two easy-to-prepare-and-good-looking-on-the-plate meals are the *Cotoletta alla Milanese* and Dad's Veal Cutlets with Mushrooms. Which leads me to Mom's first cousin, Mafalda, who lives in Bergamo, Italy, and often travels north into the Alps to spend time in the family's ancestral village of Schilpario. Mafalda is a world-class cook whose meals I would put up against any trained chef's. This veal cutlet recipe is hers.

Mafalda's Cotoletta alla Milanese (Breaded Veal Cutlet)
SERVES 4

4 pieces of veal cut in scaloppine style, weighing about ¼ pound each
2 eggs, beaten
Dried bread crumbs, using plain bread
⅓ cup butter
Salt and freshly ground black pepper
1 lemon, quartered

Flatten the veal with a mallet. Dip each piece into the beaten egg and then the bread crumbs.

Melt the butter in a large skillet and fry the veal for 2 to 3 minutes on each side until the pieces brown.

Move to a warmed serving dish and season with salt and pepper. Serve with the lemon wedges.

COOKING WITH MY SISTERS

Dad's Veal Cutlets with Mushrooms

SERVES 4 TO 6

6 veal cutlets
4 teaspoons flour
⅓ cup olive oil
6 tablespoons butter
½ cup half-and-half
½ cup dry white vermouth or Marsala wine
2 garlic cloves, minced
2 tablespoons capers, drained
4 cups fresh mushrooms, sliced
Salt and freshly ground black pepper to taste

Preheat the oven to 300 degrees.

Pound the cutlets until thin, then dust with the flour. In a large skillet, heat the olive oil. When the oil is hot, brown the cutlets on either side. Remove and place the cutlets in an 8 × 10-inch glass dish.

Drain the oil from the skillet, then stir in the butter, half-and-half, and white vermouth until well blended. Add the garlic, capers, and fresh mushrooms and cook until the mushrooms soften. Season with salt and pepper. Pour the mixture over the browned cutlets in the dish and bake for 40 minutes, or until bubbly. Delicious over rice.

Another of Mom's practices that we've all absorbed is making sure there is more than enough food to go around. Mom always says that if you leave her house hungry, it's your own fault. And that is a key admonition, uttered out loud or not, in most
Italian-American homes. The worst blunder a host or hostess can make is to appear stingy when it comes to the amount of food provided for dinner guests. That's why we prepare extra portions and servings; you can always freeze the remainder or enjoy the leftovers during the next few days. Besides the tomato sauce, one dish that's easy to make in a large batch is sausage and peppers.

Sausage and Peppers

SERVES 8

3 pounds Italian sausage, mild or hot, cut into large (3- to 4-inch) chunks
8 green peppers, sliced into wide strips
2 large onions, sliced
Salt and freshly ground black pepper to taste

Using a bit of water and just the fat from the sausage itself, cook sausage in a skillet. Just before it begins to brown, add the vegetables and season with the salt and pepper.

Serve with a good, hearty bread and a salad.

When we serve pasta, we like to have meat as a side dish. Two of our favorites are braciole and steak and onions. Braciole are little rolls of meat stuffed with spices and cheese. We made them as another meat for the Basic Tomato Sauce. You will need kitchen twine to tie the braciole.

Dinner at Viola's with cousin Ralph and the neighbors, Evelyn and Verne.

COOKING WITH MY SISTERS

Braciole (for simmering in Basic Tomato Sauce)

SERVES 6 TO 8

2 pounds top round steak, ¼ inch thick, cut into 4 × 6-inch slices
2 cups chopped Italian parsley
¾ cup chopped basil
1 cup fine Seasoned Bread Crumbs (page 34)
3 tablespoons minced garlic
1 cup grated Parmigiano-Reggiano
Salt and freshly ground black pepper to taste
⅓ cup olive oil

Pound the meat to tenderize it and make thin, but avoid making holes.

Blend the parsley and the basil, then spread the mixture on the meat.

Mix the bread crumbs with the garlic and sprinkle that atop the spice mixture on the meat.

Add the cheese and salt and pepper on top of the bread-crumb mixture.

Roll the meat, tuck in the ends, and secure with twine.

Brown the meat in the olive oil over a low temperature, and turn it gently. Transfer the meat to the pot of Basic Tomato Sauce and simmer slowly for 45 to 60 minutes, until the meat is tender. Keep an eye on it, because you don't want the meat to overcook; an hour might be too long on some stoves.

To serve, remove the meat from the pot and place on a cutting board. Remove the twine and let the meat cool for about 5 minutes. Then cut the meat into 2-inch slices, like a jelly roll, and arrange on a platter by itself or with other meats from the pot of sauce.

One of our favorite childhood meals was our mother's pot roast. This one is tasty and has an Italian flair and was prepared with local southwest Virginia root vegetables, dropped off in brown bags from Mom's farmer friends in Lee County who always had plenty of their harvest to share.

Ida's Pot Roast

SERVES 10

3 cloves of garlic, minced
3 tablespoons olive oil
6 pounds pot roast meat
3 cups flour
3 large sweet potatoes, sliced
3 large potatoes, sliced
1 large red onion, quartered
Two 28-ounce cans whole crushed tomatoes
2 cups water
1 cup Chianti wine
Salt and freshly ground black pepper to taste
2 teaspoons chili pepper flakes
2 bay leaves
Sprigs of fresh parsley to garnish

In a large, deep stew pot, sauté the minced garlic in oil over medium heat on the stovetop. Dredge the roast in flour and brown on the stovetop, turning until all sides are evenly browned. Add in the potatoes and onion, crushed tomatoes, and water.

Mix gently. Pour the cup of wine and spices over the roast. Cover the pot and simmer for 2½ to 3 hours until roast is tender. Serve with sprigs of fresh parsley.

Dad's Steak and Onions

SERVES 4

2 large sweet onions, diced
6 garlic cloves, peeled and sliced thin
¼ pound bacon strips, diced; use pancetta (Italian bacon) if available
6 tablespoons olive oil
One 28-ounce can tomato purée
2 cups beef stock
1 pound beef steaks (Dad used chuck, sliced thin)
2 cups fresh white mushrooms, sliced thin
One 28-ounce can artichoke hearts, rinsed, drained, and cut into chunks
2 cups red wine
Salt and freshly ground black pepper to taste

In a heavy, deep skillet, sauté the onions, garlic, and bacon in the olive oil until translucent. Lower the heat and add the tomato purée thinned with the beef stock. Stir the mixture and let it simmer. Then add the steaks to the skillet and cook over low heat. Add the mushrooms, artichokes, and red wine. Season with salt and pepper. Lower the heat and cook, covered, for 20 minutes, or until the steaks are tender. Terrific with roasted potatoes.

> 🦋 *A Tip from Adri:* This is a great recipe when you're out of time and company is on the way. The aroma of the sautéing onion, garlic, and bacon makes the guests believe you've been cooking all day!

✦ *Mary says:* "The 'meat as a side dish' idea translates well to dinner parties for another reason. If you're serving a meat dish and one guest happens to be a vegetarian, there is enough food to offer that guest a balanced meal without the feeling, on the guest's part, that you've gone out of your way to prepare something extra."

Filetto Perfetto
Filet Mignon Lake Como Style
MAKES FOUR 8-OUNCE FILETS

For beef lovers everywhere, here is the most delicious filet mignon recipe in our family. After a trip to visit our cousins in Italy, we went into the kitchen and asked for the recipe for this dish. It takes one skillet, a few ingredients, and a few minutes to present this amazing entrée.

4 slices of bacon, chopped
1 clove of garlic, chopped fine
1 large onion, sliced
2 pounds of filet mignon (Have the butcher slice the filet 1½ inches thick)
¼ pound butter
½ cup red wine (a dry red, claret, or Chianti)

In a hot skillet, brown the chopped bacon. Add the garlic and onion until glistening. Set aside. Place the filets in the hot skillet and turn the heat up as high as you can; brown each side for about 3 to 4 minutes. Lower the heat and continue cooking the filets for 5 minutes. Melt the butter and wine in a separate pan; simmer, never boil. Pour wine and butter sauce over the filets. Top the filets with the bacon/onion/garlic mixture and cook for another minute. Serve immediately.

When Mom could get veal, she liked to make a veal roast that Grandma Lucy used to make. This was typical Lombardian fare, in which you have a butter-based broth and vegetables of the season—although Grandma Lucy used olive oil instead of butter.

Grandma Lucy's Veal Roast and Vegetables
SERVES 8

One 4-pound veal roast
15 to 20 small potatoes, peeled and halved
10 to 20 carrots, peeled but left whole
1 pound tiny, whole pearl onions, peeled and left whole
½ pound butter (2 sticks), melted

3 cups chicken broth
2 cups dry white wine (Marsala is good)
3 tablespoons rosemary, chopped
Salt and freshly ground black pepper to taste

Preheat the oven to 375 degrees.

Place the roast in the center of a large, covered roasting pan. Place the vegetables around the roast along the bottom of the pan. Pour the butter, the broth, and then the wine over the entire contents. Sprinkle the rosemary over the contents, and salt and pepper liberally. Bake covered, checking and basting frequently, for 1½ hours or until the veal and vegetables are tender.

A Tip from Pia: Make friends with the butcher at your favorite grocery store. Call ahead to order your veal roast, because the right cut of meat is not always available.

A Tip from Checka: You can substitute a pork or beef roast for the veal, which is easier on the budget!

A Tip from Adri: Order a fresh veal roast that hasn't been prepared for cooking. Ask the butcher to leave the bone in because you'll have a richer flavor. And you'll do better with your own spices.

Another Tip from Checka: You can use baby carrots, which will cook faster. Just add them around halfway through the meat's cooking time.

A Tip from Mom: If a recipe calls for ground pepper, always use fresh black peppercorns. The taste will be tangy but not too exotic or overwhelming.

It was easier to find chicken, which was also much less expensive than veal, so Mom liked to roast chicken frequently in the way she had seen Grandmom Trigiani do it.

✦ *Toni says:* "Grandmom Trigiani usually prepared small pieces of dark meat because she believed it was tastier. I agree. Of course, she would rather walk over hot coals than spend a lot of money on chicken, so the fact that dark meat is cheaper was a bonus. Mom served a mix so that everyone could find their preference."

Grandmom Trigiani's Chicken with Rosemary Potatoes
SERVES 4 TO 6

8 pieces of chicken, if using all parts; 6 if using breasts only
Salt and freshly ground black pepper to taste
½ cup plus 2 tablespoons olive oil
4 large potatoes, cut into eighths
6 to 8 sprigs of fresh rosemary, chopped

Preheat the oven to 350 degrees.

Remove the skin and fat from the chicken, then salt and pepper each piece. Heat ½ cup olive oil in a large frying pan and slowly fry the chicken pieces, turning often to prevent burning.

In a casserole dish, line up the potatoes, drizzle them with 2 tablespoons olive oil, and sprinkle with the rosemary, salt, and pepper. Bake until tender, about 30 minutes, turning frequently to make sure they don't stick.

Turn off the oven and place the chicken in the casserole dish with the potatoes. Let sit for 10 to 15 minutes. Serve.

Grandmom Trigiani was the queen of chicken recipes. We were used to her stories about how, as a girl on the farm, she and her five brothers and sisters learned to make use of *every* part of an animal. So, as we ate her delicious chicken, she regaled us with stories of the fine art of neck-wringing—of the chickens, of course. It's amazing that we're not all vegetarians.

Grandmom made one of her favorite chicken dishes, Chicken and Polenta, whenever the local parish priests came for dinner. Polenta became an Italian staple several centuries back, when corn was taken to Italy from the New World. Food historians say that polenta got many an Italian peasant family through the winter. (Grandma Lucy liked to get fresh sausage, boil it, and serve it plain with the polenta—no gravy or sauce.) Polenta sticks to your ribs, that's for sure. And you either love it or you hate it.

Grandmom Trigiani's Chicken and Polenta
SERVES 4 TO 6

THE SAUCE
3 cups of Basic Tomato Sauce (page 31)
3 cinnamon sticks or 2 teapoons ground cinnamon

Heat the sauce in a large saucepan. Stir in the cinnamon and let the sauce simmer while the chicken is cooking.

THE CHICKEN
3 tablespoons olive oil
8 chicken pieces, with bone (4 thighs, 4 legs)
Salt and freshly ground black pepper to taste

Drizzle the olive oil in a heated frying pan. Add the chicken and sprinkle with salt and pepper. Slowly cook the chicken; do not allow a crust to form. Cook thoroughly and when finished, add directly to the tomato sauce. Let simmer for a couple of hours.

> *A Tip from Toni:* This recipe really does taste better if you use dark meat. It's fine, though, if you prefer white meat (like Mary).

THE POLENTA

(You can generally follow the instructions on any polenta package and you'll do just fine.)

6 cups water

1 teaspoon salt

2 tablespoons olive oil or butter

2 cups cornmeal or polenta meal

Bring the water to a boil, then add the salt and olive oil or butter. Pour the cornmeal into the water slowly, stirring constantly—you don't want lumps. Keep stirring until the mixture thickens.

To serve, prepare individual servings in the kitchen. Spoon the polenta on a dish and add a couple pieces of chicken with sauce. Put extra sauce on the table in case a guest likes a little extra.

A Tip from Toni: Try a double boiler. You can leave the polenta over the water and while you have to continue stirring it, you don't have to stand there for an hour.

A Tip from Mom: Buy coarse-ground cornmeal and make the polenta the old-fashioned way, stirred slowly; it's better. A lot of restaurants serve a watery, pale concoction that they call polenta, and it just doesn't hold up to many sauces. For example, this dish requires a hearty consistency in order to support the flavor of this special sauce.

Another Tip from Mom: And, if you'd like a truly authentic experience, remove the polenta from the pot, place it on a cutting board, and bring it to the table. Let it harden a bit. Then "cut" the portions using a baking string or even a heavy sewing thread. That's how Grandma Lucy used to serve it.

The Trigianis made a killer *lasagne*, which is definitely the working woman's friend. This dish can be assembled in about an hour, especially if you use precooked noodles; you can refrigerate the lasagne to bake and eat the next day, or freeze it for even later. Just thaw, then bake it in the oven for an hour, and it's truly a perfect weekday meal as well as a nice, separate course in a dinner party or on the dinner buffet.

Trigiani Lasagne with Meat and Cheese

MAKES 9 ENTRÉE PORTIONS OR 12 SIDE PORTIONS

SAUCE
4 garlic cloves, finely chopped
2 tablespoons olive oil
3½ cups crushed tomatoes
12 fresh basil leaves, finely chopped
Salt and freshly ground black pepper to taste

Combine the ingredients in a medium saucepan and simmer until the tomatoes have liquefied, 20 to 30 minutes.

A party in Grandmom's basement. Italian-Americans love to give parties in their basements and garages. Please don't ask why.

Grandmom's dining room, the site of many a fabulous meal.

RICOTTA CHEESE FILLING

15 to 16 ounces ricotta cheese

5 ounces shredded Parmigiano-Reggiano

4 ounces bread crumbs

½ teaspoon salt

4 to 5 sprigs of Italian parsley, finely chopped

While the sauce is simmering, mix the ingredients for the filling and set aside.

MEAT*

1 pound very lean ground beef

Salt and freshly ground black pepper to taste

Brown the ground beef, season with salt and pepper, and drain to practically dry. Set aside.

PASTA

12 lasagne, either oven-ready noodles or precooked

---

* If you prefer, you can alter this to include ground veal and/or ground sausage. We always use ground beef.

SPRINKLING CHEESE*

10 ounces shredded mozzarella
5 ounces shredded Parmigiano-Reggiano

Preheat the oven to 350 degrees.

Coat a large roasting pan or lasagne pan with olive oil, lightly.

Assemble the lasagne as follows:

> *Layer of pasta*
> *Thin layer of sauce*
> *Meat*
> *5 ounces mozzarella*
> *Ricotta cheese filling*
> *5 ounces Parmigiano-Reggiano*
> *Layer of pasta*
> *Thin layer of sauce*
> *5 ounces mozzarella*

Bake for one hour, covered. Remove from the oven and allow to cool for 5 to 10 minutes. Slice into squares and serve.

Trigiani Lasagne with Vegetables and Cheese
MAKES 9 ENTRÉE PORTIONS OR 12 SIDE PORTIONS

SAUCE
4 garlic cloves, finely chopped
2 tablespoons olive oil
3½ cups crushed tomatoes
12 basil leaves, finely chopped
Salt and freshly ground black pepper to taste

Combine the ingredients in a medium saucepan, and simmer until the tomatoes have liquefied, 20 to 30 minutes.

---

* While mozzarella is the traditional cheese for sprinkling, you can use almost any cheese that shreds and holds its shape. Asiago is a great example.

RICOTTA CHEESE FILLING

15 to 16 ounces ricotta cheese

5 ounces shredded Parmigiano-Reggiano

12 ounces artichoke hearts (if canned, drain)

¼ cup olive oil

½ small jar capers, drained (about 4 ounces)

Juice of 1 fresh lemon

4 ounces bread crumbs

½ teaspoon salt

While sauce is simmering, mix the ingredients for the filling and set aside.

VEGETABLES*

About 24 fresh baby spinach leaves, uncooked

1 broccoli crown, chopped and uncooked

PASTA

12 lasagne, either oven-ready noodles or precooked

SPRINKLING CHEESE**

10 ounces shredded mozzarella

5 ounces shredded Parmigiano-Reggiano

Preheat the oven to 350 degrees.

Coat a large roasting pan or lasagne pan with olive oil, lightly.

Assemble the lasagne as follows:

Layer of pasta

Thin layer of sauce

Vegetables

5 ounces mozzarella

*You can use just about anything here; already-cooked zucchini and carrots are good in this recipe, for example.

**While mozzarella is the traditional cheese for sprinkling, you can use almost any cheese that shreds and holds its shape. Asiago is a great example.

Ricotta cheese filling
5 ounces Parmigiano-Reggiano
Layer of pasta
Thin layer of sauce
5 ounces mozzarella

Bake for 1 hour, covered. Remove from the oven and allow to cool for 5 to 10 minutes. Slice into squares and serve.

> 🦋 *A Tip from Mary:* Make the lasagne for evening meetings or luncheons in your home. I have served this on a buffet to my book club, and I generally make both the meat and the vegetable versions. This is also easy to eat on your lap; no knife required. And you don't need bread; just a salad, and you're set.

Penne Alla Roseto, in the Barese Tradition

SERVES 4 TO 6

1 pound of penne (follow instructions—prepare al dente!)

SAUCE
3 cloves garlic
¼ cup extra virgin olive oil
4 anchovy fillets
1 cup bread crumbs

Freshly grated Pecorino Romano cheese to taste
Fresh parsley to garnish

As your pasta is boiling, chop the garlic and sauté in olive oil. Chop the anchovy fillets and throw into the garlic and olive oil mixture. Stir gently until the anchovies dissolve and the garlic becomes glassy. Slowly fold in the bread crumbs until browned. Drain pasta. Toss sauce through the pasta, top with cheese, garnish with parsley, and serve.

COOKING WITH MY SISTERS

Roseto, Valfortore, Italy, today.

Sometimes I add fresh peas to the sauce recipe (1 cup is plenty); if you love mushrooms, throw in a cup sliced; if you are an olive lover, throw in a cup of green and black mixed; two cups of cooked shrimp is a great addition. Have fun! And don't be afraid of the anchovies, the perfect Barese touch—light and salty, and they give the sauce a kick!

Delabole Farm Macaroni

SERVES 4 TO 6

1 pound of macaroni (your choice)
1 bag frozen peas (or 1 pound of fresh peas)
¼ pound salted butter
½ cup shredded Parmigiano-Reggiano
½ teaspoon salt
¼ cup olive oil (to drizzle)
1 bunch of fresh mint
Juice of ½ lemon
½ teaspoon freshly ground black pepper or ½ teaspoon red pepper flakes
    (your choice)
1 cup finely grated Parmigiano-Reggiano

Boil the macaroni following package directions. When the pasta is nearly done al dente, throw in the peas. Boil peas with the pasta for a minute.

Drain pasta and peas (never rinse!) and set aside.

Throw the butter on top of the pasta and peas. Sprinkle the shredded cheese with ½ teaspoon of salt and toss until the butter has melted through. Drizzle the mixture with ¼ cup of olive oil.

Tear up and add the fresh mint (leaving a few pretty leaves for garnish to the side), squeeze the juice of ½ fresh lemon on the pasta, add the pepper of your choice, and toss through the pasta and peas. Before serving, garnish with the grated cheese and a sprig of mint. It never hurts to give the finished dish a splash of olive oil before serving.

Rigatoni Dolce

SERVES 4 TO 6

3 large baked sweet potatoes or 6 small baked sweet potatoes
(You need about 3 cups)
1 tablespoon honey
4 cloves of garlic, minced
1 tablespoon butter
1 cup grated Parmigiano-Reggiano
1 box of rigatoni
Salt to taste
(Adriana's favorite additional options below!)

In advance, bake the sweet potatoes. Preheat the oven to 375 degrees. Wash and puncture the sweet potatoes, roll in tin foil, and bake for one hour or until tender. Scoop the meat out of the skins, drizzle with the honey, and mash lightly with a fork (you want your sweet potatoes chunky, not smooth!).

In a skillet, glaze the garlic in a pat of butter, until garlic is glassy. Fold in the baked potatoes, sprinkle with a teaspoon or so of the grated cheese, and set aside.

Prepare the rigatoni per package instructions. Place the drained, hot rigatoni in a serving dish, sprinkle with grated cheese, and toss until the rigatoni is covered with the cheese.

Spoon the sweet potato mixture on top of the rigatoni and toss. Sprinkle with grated cheese, add salt to taste, and serve!

OPTIONS: Sometimes I throw pignoli nuts in with the sweet potatoes, sometimes I throw chopped scallions on top! I throw 2 cups of kale in with the garlic and butter until it wilts, or I throw a handful of fresh sage until it wilts. Add whatever YOU like to the base recipe!

Another solid dinner dish is Mom's stuffed peppers. These are truly delicious; they also look pretty on a plate and balance well with a salad, potatoes, or rice. And stuffed peppers work well as a course following soup or a large antipasto, before an elaborate dessert.

Mom's Stuffed Peppers

SERVES 4 (IF EVERYONE EATS 2)

THE FILLING

1 pound ground beef, browned
1 tablespoon minced garlic
1 cup fine bread crumbs
¼ cup grated Parmigiano-Reggiano
4 tablespoons chopped Italian parsley
3 fresh basil leaves, finely chopped
1 cup fresh tomatoes, precooked (or canned tomatoes)
2 eggs
4 tablespoons olive oil
8 medium peppers, stemmed, cored, and seeded
1 tablespoon olive oil for drizzling over peppers before baking
1 cup Basic Tomato Sauce (page 31)

Preheat the oven to 400 degrees.

Combine the beef with all the other filling ingredients, then stuff the peppers all the way to the top. It's fine if the peppers bulge a bit.

Stand the peppers on end in a casserole dish and drizzle the olive oil over them. Bake at 400 degrees for 15 minutes, then reduce the temperature to 375 degrees and pour the tomato sauce around them. Continue baking until the peppers brown, about 30 minutes. Bring to the table in the casserole dish and serve.

A Tip from Pia: Mom sometimes made these with rice in the mixture. It makes the dish a bit heartier.

But the best thing about the stuffed peppers is that telling you about them, and all these other delightful dishes, brings me back to my mom's kitchen.

I remember fall days in Big Stone Gap, when we would run home to be on time for dinner, and there was enough of a nip in the air that the kitchen window was fogged up from whatever Mom was cooking. Over dinner we would tell stories and strengthen our ties to one another. And this was all possible because Mom's kitchen was warm, inviting, creative, and reminiscent of all of the kitchens in the family that came before ours.

At Grandmom and Grandpop's.

Light Suppers

Adri, Toni, and Tom Bean picnic in the Cumberland Gap.

randma Lucy and Grandmom Trigiani had different approaches to meat and cheese and pasta and sauce, but they shared a dedication to doing things well. Every woman in our family still enjoys the praise that greets us when we enter the dining room with platters of luscious pasta, well-seasoned meats, and colorful side dishes. Whatever we accomplish in our careers or communities, the perfect meatball will most likely be our legacy.

Grandma Lucy took pleasure in precision, Grandmom Trigiani in speed and economy. Mom emphasized an orderly environment, and Dad's priority was dinner on the table the moment he was ready to sit down.

Enter the light supper. On the nights that we all had to go somewhere — a football or basketball game, a concert, or a production of the Big Stone Gap Music Club — or on those evenings when Mom and Dad were going out as a duo, Mom would make something that she could pull together quickly.

In the event that the entire family was going out to a performance of some kind, the light-supper approach worked well for another reason: it wasn't sleep-inducing. Unless you were Dad.

In the seventies, the community leaders of Big Stone Gap signed a contract with a concert organization to sponsor four events per year. You joined the local association and purchased tickets for the events. They usually offered a variety of entertainments, from Broadway to classical, performed by traveling troupes of professional artists.

In the ongoing effort to expose us to different cultural happenings, Mom and Dad joined. (Eventually, Mom even helped to coordinate the program.) Community Concert nights were light-supper nights because we had to get there on time. It's important to note here that Dad's work day started at seven a.m. so he was usually up by five. (He never missed a sunrise if he could help it. It was his favorite time of day.) And even though Dad always took a catnap during the afternoon, he usually was pretty tired by dinnertime. Those concerts were a real sacrifice for him on some nights. So much so that it was a struggle for him to stay awake, particularly during the classical offerings. But Dad never skipped a performance.

One evening, we took up our usual row of seats in the high school auditorium. A woodwind quartet was in performance that night. Mom went in first, then the seven of us, girls first, then boys, and, finally, Dad on the other end. About a third of the way through the concert, Dad hit full REM sleep, and he began to snore. Michael and Carlo thought it was hysterical, as did most of the men in the audience. We didn't tell Mom for a while, but then the snoring got so loud she could hear it, and she sent word down the line that someone needed to poke Dad. The boys pleaded temporary deafness and the snoring continued until Mom gave one of her looks — translation: Do it or suffer the consequences. From that point on, if Dad started nodding off, someone brought him back to the living.

But Dad loved entertainment of virtually any kind. He began playing the piano when he was three years old. He was a natural musician, jazzy and improvisational. Dad was especially popular with the manager of the piano store in the mall over in Kingsport, Tennessee. (He should have received a commission for the pianos sold due to his demos.)

✦ *Mary says:* "Dad knew how to read music, but he played the piano without it. I remember standing by the piano bench, barely tall enough to reach the keyboard, and watching Dad play. He was truly happy in those moments, completely absorbed in the rhythm and relaxation of making the music. It's what made me want to learn to play."

✦ *Toni says:* "I remember that Dad played almost every night after coming home from work, just before dinner. I loved to listen."

✦ *Checka says:* "Dad would play anywhere there was a piano — restaurants, friends' homes, schools, even hospitals!"

We sang in church, and by the early 1970s, the guitar Mass was all the rage. I was always jealous of the Baptists, who still had enthusiastic choirs. We Catholics were holding hands around the campfire.

✦ *Pia says:* "Our arrival in Big Stone Gap happened after Vatican Two, so things were beginning to loosen up. Except at our house. For years we continued to eat fish on Fridays, and all the girls were required to wear something on our heads for Mass on Sunday. So we used these little chapel veils — circles of lace that looked like doilies. We had four white ones and one black one, and we fought over the black one every Sunday because it was the least conspicuous on our brunette heads. Adri, though, would fold and fold and fold the chapel veil until it was the size of a minuscule piece of pie and attach it to the top of her head with a bobby pin."

We were very proud when Mom would make one of her colorful *antipasti* for church gatherings, but we loved to have them at home, all to ourselves. Mom had learned to make this dish when she married Dad. The *antipasto* is the first, or appetizer, course in Italian cuisine. The course begins the meal by introducing a variety of tastes, awakening the palate to what will follow. In Italy, the contents of the antipasto vary from season to season, depending on what is available, and the course is often served buffet-style, with many separate offerings. In Roseto, Pennsylvania, the plated antipasto often includes garden vegetables canned for use throughout the year, and the hostess served the antipasto with drinks while dinner was cooking. Either way, it's easy to do and doesn't involve any cooking. It's perfect if you're hosting guests for cocktails before dinner out.

Antipasto

SERVES 6 FOR DINNER, 10 FOR APPETIZERS

Romaine lettuce (usually only 1 head, have another just in case)
Two 16-ounce cans white albacore tuna packed in water
9 hard-boiled eggs, sliced in half
One 15-ounce jar roasted red peppers
Two 4-ounce cans anchovies rolled with capers
8 ounces pitted black olives
8 ounces pitted green olives
½ pound Genoa salami, sliced thin and rolled *
½ pound prosciutto, sliced very thin and rolled
One 12-ounce can artichoke hearts
One 7-ounce can mushrooms packed in olive oil
½ pound Cheddar cheese sliced in ½ × 2-inch strips**
½ pound Monterey Jack cheese sliced in ½ × 2-inch strips**
12 ounces pepperoncini peppers
Fresh Italian parsley, for garnish
Olive oil, for drizzling

* Other meats we've used: cotto salami, capicola, soppressata.

** You can go for more authentic Italian cheeses; we use the "American" varieties for color.

Christmas on the farm.

The key to this recipe is to make the platter attractive and artistic. Line a 12-inch platter (we like a round shape) with the larger lettuce leaves, which will serve as the base of the antipasto as well as a way to measure a portion. (Ideally, a person should be able to pull a whole lettuce leaf off the finished antipasto with a little of everything on top.) In the center of the platter place the tuna; it's best to use a canned variety so that you can turn the can upside down and remove the tuna intact, retaining the shape of the can. Add the roasted red peppers and place them around the platter in a symmetrical pattern, like the rays of the sun. Continue in the same pattern with the remaining ingredients until the tray is covered and all ingredients have been used. Drizzle with olive oil and serve.

> *A Tip from Mary:* Fresh ingredients are wonderful for this dish, and you can make this ultra-fancy by preparing your own tuna, roasting fresh bell peppers, buying imported olives, and using only Italian cheeses. But if you go to an Italian specialty store and buy products prepared in Italy, you'll make a fine antipasto. And when it comes to the tuna, don't drain it too excessively; you want a little of the flavor that comes from the oil.

Happy IBM (Italian By Marriage) Husband Salad

SERVES 4 TO 6

SALAD

4 cups fresh baby spinach, rinsed, patted dry, lightly salted
2 grapefruits (sectioned and deseeded)
1 red onion, chopped fine
6 figs, quartered (leave skins and seeds, remove the stem)
¼ cup chopped walnuts
½ cup mascarpone cheese
Salt and freshly ground black pepper to taste

DRESSING

2 tablespoons honey
3 tablespoons olive oil
¼ cup Parmigiano-Reggiano, grated fine
⅓ cup balsamic vinegar
Juice of one fresh lemon

In a trifle bowl or a clear glass bowl, place one layer of spinach, follow with a layer of sectioned grapefruit, add another layer of spinach, add a layer of onion, another layer of spinach, and a layer of figs. Sprinkle chopped walnuts on top of the figs. Set aside and prepare the dressing.

To make the dressing, warm the honey, olive oil, grated cheese, and balsamic vinegar on the stove. Whisk gently until relatively smooth (do not boil). Drizzle salad with fresh lemon juice followed by the warm dressing, dollop with mascarpone cheese, season with salt and pepper, and serve immediately.

Another of Mom's light dishes was her version of *pasta fazool* ("when the stars make you drool just like pasta fazool"), known as *pasta e fagioli* in Italian.

COOKING WITH MY SISTERS

Pasta e Fagioli

SERVES 8

3 cups cooked cannellini (white kidney) beans
10 cups water
Salt to taste
1 cup olive oil
1 onion, chopped
2 tablespoons chopped Italian parsley
4 cups cooked pasta (broken pieces of large noodles or a small noodle such as orecchiette)
¼ cup grated Parmigiano-Reggiano or Romano
Freshly ground black pepper to taste

In a large saucepan, combine the beans, water, salt, oil, onion, and parsley. Bring to a boil, then lower the heat and simmer for 20 minutes, or until the beans are tender. Add the pasta and allow to simmer another 10 minutes.

Toss the beans and pasta together in a large bowl with the cheese. Salt and pepper to taste. Serve in bowls and sprinkle with cheese.

> *A Tip from Checka:* My kids like good old canned baked beans in tomato sauce mixed with elbow macaroni. It's not authentic, but it's still pasta and beans!

Ida's Easy Artichoke and Chicken Casserole

SERVES 6 TO 8

Great for potlucks or cook-ahead meals, and a great first casserole for children to make, this one is from our mom!

Three 9-ounce packages of cooked chicken strips (white meat)
3 cans artichoke hearts, quartered
3 cups white mushrooms, sliced thin
1 fresh lemon

2 cloves of garlic, minced
1 teaspoon capers
½ cup gluten-free "bread" crumbs (or use regular if you wish)
½ cup Parmigiano-Reggiano, grated
½ cup olive oil

Preheat the oven to 350 degrees.

In a 9-by-12-inch glass baking dish, toss in the chicken, artichokes, and mushrooms. Squeeze with the juice of one fresh lemon. Toss in the garlic, capers, bread crumbs (leave aside about ¼ cup for topping), and cheese, drizzle with olive oil, then mix thoroughly. Sprinkle remaining bread crumbs on top.

Bake for 45 minutes.

One of our favorites is a humble chicken and rice soup. The best one was made by Mary Falcone, Grandpop's cousin. ZiZi Mary, as we called her, always had a snack for us when we went to visit. We've recreated the chicken and rice soup recipe here, but we can't guarantee that it will ever be the same as when that wonderful lady welcomed us into her home. There was something about her and the snow globe in her parlor and the picture of her son, Tommy (which always made her cry because he was lost in the Pacific during the Second World War), that made her house so comfortable and warm. As our family got bigger, ZiZi Mary was one of the people who could make you feel like you were the only kid in the world. Her home was a bit of a refuge, and her soup its everlasting symbol.

ZiZi Mary's Chicken and Rice Soup
SERVES 8

1 plump 4- to 5-pound chicken, cut into pieces
Salt and freshly ground black pepper to taste
6 quarts cold water
4 cups cooked rice; if using Arborio, follow the directions for risotto
¼ cup chopped Italian parsley

Place the chicken, salt, and pepper in a large pot containing the water. Bring to a boil, then lower the heat and simmer for about 2 hours. The broth is done when the meat is falling off the bone. Remove the meat and bones, reserving the meat for another dish. If you are serving this as a lunch entrée, you can leave some meat in the broth.

Add the rice and simmer for 30 to 45 minutes on very low heat. Add the parsley just before serving.

We used to visit our grandmothers during the summer break. As teenagers, we called Grandmom Trigiani's house "Camp Viola," since outdoor groundskeeping and indoor bleaching were on the duty chart. Our visits tested not just her patience with children but her ability to stretch a dollar to infinitesimal lengths. Her minestrone made good use of leftovers. And it's great any time of the year. Try to make the beef broth one day ahead.

Grandmom Trigiani's Minestrone
SERVES 12 TO 16

1 medium onion, chopped
2 garlic cloves, minced
1 large carrot, chopped
2 tablespoons olive oil
6 cups Beef Broth (recipe follows)
3 cups water
3 basil leaves, chopped
1/4 teaspoon freshly ground black pepper
One 28-ounce can tomatoes, crushed, or 1 pint home-canned tomatoes
One 19-ounce can white pinto beans, rinsed and drained
1 cup peas
1 cup small pasta, uncooked (equivalent of about 3 servings)
1/2 cup Parmigiano-Reggiano, grated

In a large saucepan, sauté the onion, garlic, and carrot in the olive oil until the garlic and onion are soft. Add the broth, water, basil, and pepper. Bring to a boil. Add the tomatoes, beans, peas, and pasta. Reduce the heat and simmer for about 2 hours.

Serve with the cheese on the side.

Beef Broth

2½ pounds beef (brisket or shank)
1 shank bone
6 quarts water
Salt and freshly ground black pepper

Combine the ingredients in a large stockpot, bringing the water to a boil. At
that point, skim the top and lower the heat to a simmer. Cook for 2 to 3 hours,
adding salt and pepper to taste. Then strain the broth, saving the meat either for
the soup or for another purpose. Refrigerate the broth. The next day, skim the
congealed fat from the top.

Big Stone Gap Baptist Church Supper Ham and Rice Casserole

SERVES 8

4 cups cooked wild rice (You can substitute brown rice, quinoa,
  white rice—whatever you like)

½ cup green peppers, diced
½ cup red peppers, diced
½ cup yellow peppers, diced
½ cup celery, diced
1 cup red onion, diced
4 tablespoons butter

2 tablespoons flour
2 cups evaporated milk
2 cups baked ham, cut in julienne strips
1 teaspoon dry mustard

1 teaspoon garlic salt
¼ teaspoon red pepper
1 teaspoon Worcestershire sauce
2 cups grated sharp Cheddar cheese

Preheat the oven to 350 degrees. Set aside the cooked rice. On the stovetop, sauté the peppers, celery, and red onion in 4 tablespoons of butter until tender. Set aside. In a separate pan, make a roux with the flour and milk until the sauce is thick, stirring constantly. Add the cooked rice, vegetables, roux, and ham together in a large bowl, stirring until well mixed. Season mixture with dry mustard, garlic salt, red pepper, and Worcestershire sauce. Blend well. Place mixture in a casserole dish and sprinkle with the Cheddar cheese. Bake for 35 to 40 minutes or until cheese is bubbly.

One summer, I decided I wanted a little more cash than what Viola would dole out for us to put in the Sunday-morning collection plate, so that's when I took a job at the Mount Bethel Inn. I'd often get home late, and Grandmom would whip up a delicious quick meal. What I came to call Venetian Eggs was my favorite.

Grandmom's Venetian Eggs
SERVES 4

DRESSING FOR GREENS
1 cup balsamic vinegar
2 tablespoons fresh lemon juice
Salt and freshly ground black pepper to taste

4 cups Basic Tomato Sauce (page 31)
4 eggs
4 cups fresh arugula
4 cups baby spinach

In a small bowl, whisk the ingredients for the dressing until well combined.

Ladle the tomato sauce into a large skillet. Heat over medium and when the sauce begins to bubble at the edges of the pan, make a well in the sauce with a spoon. Crack an egg into the well. Follow suit with the rest of the eggs.

Toss the arugula and spinach in a large bowl with the dressing. Place the greens on plates. When the eggs are cooked to your preference (soft, medium, or well done), use a spatula to place an egg and some sauce over the greens, tossing lightly.

The Roseto-style tomato pie (focaccia) is a great stand-alone dish, or you can serve it with soup or eggs. This pizza, with a thin but chewy crust and sweetened tomato sauce that soaks into the top and is dusted lightly with finely grated cheese, is terrific with a salad and nothing else.

Pizze

MAKES ONE 12-INCH RECTANGULAR PIZZA; SERVES 8 TO 12
DEPENDING ON THE SIZE OF THE PIECES

BASIC PIZZA DOUGH
1 tablespoon active dry yeast
¾ cup warm water
Pinch of sugar
2½ cups unbleached all-purpose flour
3 tablespoons olive oil
1 teaspoon salt

In a small mixing bowl, dissolve the yeast in the warm water with the sugar. Set aside for 5 minutes.

On a large, flat surface, pour the flour into a mound, shaping a large well in the center. Pour the yeast mixture, 1 tablespoon of the olive oil, and the salt into the well. Then slowly work the flour into the center, using your fingers. Begin forming the mixture into a ball, kneading it until the dough can stretch. This takes between 10 and 15 minutes. Keep a little warm water close by, using a little at a time in case you need it to work the dough. The dough should always be soft but not wet.

Place the ball of dough into a large mixing bowl that you've coated lightly with olive oil. Turn the ball over until it's covered with the oil. Then cover the bowl with a clean dish towel. Put the dough in a warm place, away from any drafts, to rise. In about an hour and a half, it should be double its original size. At that point, it's ready to bake.

Preheat the oven to 425 degrees. Remove the dough from the bowl and knead it again for 5 minutes. Roll out the dough to about half the size of a 12- to 14-inch pizza pan. Lightly coat the pan with olive oil, then place the dough in the pan and spread it evenly to the edges. Your goal should be to have the pizza no more than ¼ inch thick.

Design your pizza, then bake it for about 30 minutes. When the crust is brown, remove it from the oven and serve it immediately.

TOMATO PIES A LA ROSETO (FOCACCIA)

1 small onion, very finely chopped
3 tablespoons olive oil
One 15-ounce can tomatoes, drained and crushed
1 teaspoon sugar
5 fresh basil leaves
Salt and freshly ground black pepper to taste
1 sheet of prepared Basic Pizza Dough (page 96)
½ cup grated Romano cheese

In a medium skillet, sauté the onion in the olive oil until it is very soft. In a large saucepan, combine the onion with the tomatoes, sugar, basil, salt, and pepper. Cook over low heat until the sauce is very thick, 20 to 30 minutes.

Preheat the oven to 425 degrees.

Using a ladle, spoon the sauce over the pizza dough. Spread it evenly. Sprinkle with the cheese.

Bake for about 25 minutes, or until the edges are brown.

> *A Tip from Checka:* To make a pizza quickly, use a prepared crust or a dough mix. Usually, the local pizza joint is happy to oblige.

Light suppers, light hearts, loose pants, I like to say. Here's to limitless variations!

CHAPTER FIVE

On the Side

Sidekicks: Francesca and Carlo.

The best lesson we learned from the great cooks of our family is: Keep it simple.

Make the most of your time and effort.

Take care of your guests.

Let the food shine.

In our world, this devotion to simplicity extended to everything we did. Yet even the most humble of vegetables got a dash of star treatment. Take Grandma Lucy's trick with carrots.

Grandma Lucy's Sweet Carrots
SERVES 6 TO 8

1 pound baby carrots, peeled and cleaned
2 tablespoons granulated sugar
Salt and freshly ground black pepper to taste
Butter to taste

In a saucepan, cover the carrots with water. Stir in the sugar and bring to a boil. Cook until tender, then strain. Add the salt, pepper, and butter.

Then there were Grandma Lucy's potatoes, which she boiled with the skins on, then peeled and quartered. She liked to work with potatoes that way because she felt they stayed firmer and held their shape.

Grandma Lucy's Quartered Potatoes
SERVES 8

10 medium-size red potatoes
¼ cup olive oil
⅛ cup vinegar
½ cup chopped onion
Salt and freshly ground black pepper to taste

Boil the potatoes whole and unpeeled. When done, drain and remove to a bowl, allowing to cool for 5 to 10 minutes. While still warm, peel off the skins, then quarter the potatoes. If the quarters are too large, cut in half.
    Add all the other ingredients and toss. Serve.

> *A Tip from Checka:* Balsamic vinegar adds a different twist to any dish calling for vinegar, but it's not an absolute necessity. Rumor has it that we use more of it in this country than they do in Italy!

Grandmom Trigiani would do a great turn with the equally humble green bean. She glamorized it with the Basic Tomato Sauce.

Grandmom Trigiani's Green Beans in Tomato Sauce

SERVES 4

2 cups fresh green beans
3 tablespoons olive oil
1 cup Basic Tomato Sauce (page 31)
Salt and freshly ground black pepper to taste

Snip the ends of the beans and wash them thoroughly. Drizzle the olive oil in a frying pan. Pour in the tomato sauce and let it simmer. Place the beans in the sauce and allow them to simmer until they are cooked. Season with salt and pepper.

Grandmom in jet beads and emerald green enjoys scintillating conversation at dinner.

Sun. nite

Dear Adri:
Arrived home from N.Y. at 5 o'clock everything went well. Saw Rosalie and a lot of your friends all asked for you. But the highlight was this clipping from the South Bend Tribune. Aren't you proud. 5/14/82 Don't forget Ralphs Birthday. I may come to N.Y. some Saturday I must buy some clothes for all the affairs. I'll call you. Be good and don't do anything foolish.

Love Grandmom.

"Be good and don't do anything foolish." Viola Trigiani

Grandmom Trigiani loved to create special effects for her dinner parties, so we inherited several recipes for side dishes that use traditionally Italian ingredients in a decidedly fifties-era fashion. (Mary thinks this is because Grandmom's golden age was the Eisenhower era, populated with Oysters Rockefeller and cocktails, and pineapple upside-down cake and demitasses.) For her dinner parties, Grandmom liked to make a couple of fancier sides that required a little more effort than usual—such as artichokes and mushrooms. I could live on these artichokes!

Grandmom Trigiani's Stuffed Artichokes

SERVES 4

4 artichokes
4 garlic cloves
¼ cup olive oil
2 cups bread crumbs
4 ounces fresh shredded Parmigiano-Reggiano or Romano cheese (reserve a small
    amount for garnish)
One 3-ounce jar capers, drained
Juice of 1 lemon
Salt and freshly ground black pepper to taste
2 cups chicken stock

Trim the artichokes. Cut the stalk off close to the base squarely so the artichoke can sit upright. Slice the top off each artichoke and pinch out the center. With kitchen scissors, cut off the ends of *every* leaf. Place artichokes in a covered pan with about ½ inch of water and steam until they open (they should turn a beautiful rich green color), about 30 minutes.

Sauté the garlic briefly in 2 tablespoons of the oil. In a large bowl, mix the bread crumbs, garlic, cheese, capers, lemon juice, the remaining oil, and the salt and pepper. Save a small portion of cheese for garnish.

Preheat the oven to 350 degrees.

Stuff the artichokes. Hold an opened artichoke over the bowl and with a teaspoon or your hand, stuff bread-crumb mixture into every leaf you can, and particularly the center. Place the stuffed artichokes in an oven-safe pan with a lid. Pour the chicken stock over the artichokes and add enough water to have an inch of liquid on the bottom. Pour the remaining bread-crumb mixture over the artichokes and sprinkle the remaining cheese on top.

Cover and bake for about an hour. The artichokes should be about to fall apart. Serve with an extra empty bowl for the discarded leaves.

Sautéed Mushrooms

SERVES 4 TO 6

¼ pound (1 stick) butter
1 yellow onion, chopped
1 pound whole white mushrooms*
1 garlic clove, minced
½ teaspoon fresh thyme
½ teaspoon fresh oregano
½ teaspoon fresh basil
½ teaspoon salt
½ cup white wine

In a large sauté pan, heat the butter. Add the onion and sauté until golden. Add the remaining ingredients and simmer slowly for 45 minutes, or until the mushrooms are tender.

Place in a serving bowl and serve with your favorite dish. The sauce makes an excellent accompaniment for any main meat dish.

A Tip from Pia: Really make this dish pop by adding a dash of hot sauce just before removing it from the heat.

A Tip from Checka: These are great over pork or lamb chops.

* You can go more chichi here with some fancy mushrooms, but Grandmom always used plain white mushrooms.

Mom's cauliflower dish is in this mode—an extra-special treatment for a plain vegetable. This works as an appetizer, too.

Mom's Cauliflower
SERVES 6 TO 8

1 large head of cauliflower
2 eggs
2 cups all-purpose flour
1 tablespoon baking powder
2 tablespoons minced garlic
½ cup whole milk
½ cup olive oil

Clean the cauliflower. Steam the whole head until tender (or until a skewer can pierce). Do not overcook. Set aside to cool and then cut into small florets. Set aside.

In a large bowl, beat the eggs. Add the remaining ingredients except the olive oil and stir to blend well.

Heat the olive oil in a small or medium saucepan. Drag each floret through the batter, coating it evenly. Drop the florets into the hot olive oil in batches and remove when golden. Drain on paper towels.

And if Grandmom Trigiani could find blood oranges, it was a safe bet that you would be treated to the Roseto tradition of sliced oranges as prepared here. But regular oranges work just fine. And sometimes she would top them, Roseto style, with black olives for extra pizzazz.

Oranges with Cracked Pepper
SERVES 6 TO 8

3 large oranges
3 tablespoons olive oil
Freshly ground black pepper

Peel the oranges and slice about ¼ inch thick. Remove the seeds. Place the oranges on a plate and drizzle with the olive oil. Grind fresh pepper on top. Serve.

Another great appetizer or side dish was the buffalo-style mozzarella cheese served with tomatoes or roasted red bell peppers, or just with freshly ground black pepper. Grandmom Trigiani used to substitute mozzarella with a variation called *scamorza*, which she would buy fresh from the Calandra family's farm in Nazareth, Pennsylvania. Scamorza is one variety of the white cow's-milk cheeses produced in southern Italy. Another is *caciocavallo* (we won't tell you what that means). The true buffalo mozzarella, made in Italy from buffalo's milk, can be hard to find, but it's starting to be produced in the United States now. You can find scamorza in the Italian neighborhoods of some cities, and while it resembles mozzarella, scamorza has a slightly saltier, heartier flavor and heavier consistency. We love it.

Mozzarella and Tomatoes
SERVES 4 TO 6

1 pound fresh mozzarella or scamorza cheese
2 large fresh tomatoes
2 tablespoons olive oil
Salt and freshly ground black pepper to taste

Slice the cheese and tomatoes about ¼ inch thick. Place on a plate in a circular pattern. Drizzle the olive oil over the tomatoes and mozzarella and season with salt and pepper.

> *A Tip from Mary:* I prefer roasted bell peppers. Here's an easy way to do this at home.

Roasting Peppers

SERVES 4 TO 6

6 bell peppers of any color (but we like red), cored, seeded, and sliced lengthwise
Olive oil
Salt

Arrange the peppers next to each other on the rack of a broiling pan skin side up.

Broil, not too close to the heat, for about 5 minutes, or until you can see the peppers blistering. Turn them. After the other side has browned, remove them from the broiler.

Move the peppers to a closed container (it can be anything—a pan with a tight-fitting lid, a plastic bag, even a brown paper bag) to allow them to steam. After they've cooled, 10 to 15 minutes, peel or scrape the brown parts. Drizzle with olive oil and season with salt before serving. To store, place in a tightly covered container, covered with more olive oil.

For weekday dinners, Grandmom Trigiani liked to make casseroles that could be served as a side for more than one meal.

Offer to make this side dish for any potluck supper, and you'll be the queen or king of the event! Make two. Take one to the party and keep one at home for a week's worth of good, southern side eating!

St. Anthony Church Supper Baked Potato Casserole
SERVES 12 TO 14

1 large sweet onion
1 pound bacon
1 cup mayonnaise
1 cup sour cream
10 potatoes (peeled, boiled, sliced thin)
1 pound Cheddar cheese, grated

Preheat the oven to 325 degrees.

Chop the sweet onion fine. Dice the bacon and lightly brown it on the stovetop. Set aside.

Combine the mayonnaise and sour cream until well mixed. In a large, greased casserole pan, layer the potatoes, followed by a thin layer of the onion, followed by a thin layer of the cheese, dollops of the mayo/cream combo, and repeat the process until the casserole dish is filled to the top. Sprinkle the partially cooked bacon on top. Bake one hour.

Grandmom Trigiani's Asparagus Tips

SERVES 6 TO 8

20 asparagus spears, chopped into ½-inch pieces
3 ounces blue cheese, softened
8 ounces goat cheese, softened
1 egg, beaten

Preheat the oven to 400 degrees. Begin steaming the asparagus; stop when it becomes a bright, vivid green.

While the asparagus is steaming, in a large bowl blend the cheeses and the egg. Toss with the cooked asparagus. Place in a shallow baking pan, covered, and bake for 20 minutes.

Grandmom Trigiani's Baked Zucchini

SERVES 6 TO 8

1 medium onion, chopped
2 garlic cloves, minced
½ cup olive oil
3 cups zucchini, sliced thin in rounds
½ cup Parmigiano-Reggiano
4 eggs, slightly beaten
4 teaspoons chopped fresh Italian parsley

Preheat the oven to 350 degrees.

In a large skillet, brown the onion and garlic in the olive oil. Layer the zucchini in a lightly greased baking dish, sprinkling some of the onion-garlic mixture and some of the cheese over each layer. Pour the eggs over the zucchini, making sure to cover the zucchini completely. Sprinkle the parsley over the top. Bake for 40 minutes, or until lightly browned on top.

Grandma Lucy with a few grandchildren. From left, Mary Theresa, Mary Yolanda, Andrea, and Donnie.

> 🌿 *A Tip from Pia:* Don't skimp on the cheese. Use good ingredients; it makes for better flavor.

At home in Big Stone Gap, Mom always served a vegetable and a salad because she liked to make sure we got plenty of greens. Even if it was iceberg lettuce with onions, tomatoes, and green peppers, it did the trick. Mom taught us how to make and toss the salad with oil and vinegar. (Remember: more oil than vinegar.) We never saw a bottled dressing in Ida's kitchen. And, we ate our salad right on the big dinner plate.

    ✦ *Pia says:* "I'll never forget that night after Adri's 'sous chef' gig at the Mount Bethel Inn, when Mom asked her to make the salad for dinner. Everything was fine until Adri put her hands into the bowl and started tossing the salad with her fingers. I thought Mom was going to faint."

When we visited Mom's uncle, Monsignor Andrea Spada, in Bergamo, we would see the salad dressing prepared a little differently. Mom's cousin Mafalda, the marvelous cook, kept house for their uncle Don Andrea (as we called him). Mafalda, her husband, Arturo, and their children, Monica and Andrea, lived with Don Andrea in a beautiful sixteenth-century apartment above the newspaper he published. While Mafalda prepared the entire meal, she would leave the salad greens unadorned and serve them in a large bowl, and Don Andrea would dress the salad—two parts olive oil to one part vinegar, just salt and pepper—as if playing a string instrument, with both arms moving at the same pace but in opposite directions.

Mom grew up in the apartment above her parents' shoe store. Grandma Lucy's kitchen was at the top of the staircase from the ground floor, and it had a window so Lucy could see who was ascending the stairs. The kitchen was probably about twenty feet square, with a big table and comfortable chairs. Grandma Lucy had a calming presence; you could relax in her kitchen. If you were relaxing in a Trigiani kitchen, though, it meant you didn't have enough to do.

When Grandma Lucy decided to stay in America, she knew she would never see her mother again. They corresponded and even talked occasionally, once long-distance telephone calls became possible, but this was a deep sadness for her.

One night, her mother came to her in a dream. Lucy was standing at the top of the stairs to her apartment, and her mother was standing at the bottom. Lucy asked, "Mama, why are you here? I'm so happy!" And her mother said, "I came to see you." A few weeks later, Lucy received a letter from Don Andrea, with the sad news that their mother had died. He shared very specific details, including the time and date of her death. Lucy noted with shock that her mother died the night of her dream.

But our visits to Bergamo and Schilpario made Grandma Lucy happy. We would tell her all about her nieces and nephews, and their children, and our adventures. And the food always figured into the stories.

Of course, one of the all-time best side dishes in Bergamo was Mafalda's *risotto alla Milanese*, made with precious saffron and, often, mushrooms. On my first visit there, after college, the only thing I could muster in Italian was *"Italia Oggi,"* the title of my college Italian textbook. After my siblings and parents expressed their embarrassment, Mafalda took me under her wing and was most patient in attempting to communicate with me. This risotto crossed all language barriers, though.

✦ *Toni says:* "There's a better story than that about Adri's Italian, or lack thereof. Mom, Adri, Tim, Lucia, and I were in Italy in 2003, getting ready to return to the U.S. from Milan. We were at the airport, and a nice guy was helping us, and thinking she was saying, 'You're the man, you're the man,' Adri kept saying, 'Tu sei il mano, tu sei il mano.' (Actually, it would be *la* mano, but this story is not about grammar.) Because *mano* means *hand* in Italian, Adri was actually saying, 'You're the hand, you're the hand.'"

A Tip from Adri: My memory of childhood is that we ate everything on a plant except the stems. One of my favorite summer dishes was zucchini flowers and in the fall, pumpkin blossoms. Both are prepared in a similar fashion. Some folks add cheese to the center, but for me, that's gilding the blossom. When you make these, you will understand why!

Gram's Zucchini Flowers or Pumpkin Blossoms
SERVES 8

16 pumpkin blossoms or 16 zucchini flowers
1 cup bread crumbs
2 basil leaves, chopped fine
4 sprigs of parsley, chopped fine
1 tablespoon grated Romano cheese
Salt and freshly ground black pepper to taste
2 eggs, beaten
6 tablespoons fresh cream
1 cup flour
2 cups olive oil
1 fresh lemon

Wash the flowers or the blossoms, removing any stems. Set aside.

Combine the bread crumbs, basil, parsley, Romano cheese, and salt and pepper. Beat the eggs and add cream until well blended. Set up a station with a bowl with the eggs and cream, a cookie sheet with the flour, and finally a bowl with the bread crumbs and herbs.

Heat the olive oil in a small skillet on the stove until bubbly. Have another cookie sheet lined with a paper towel to drain the fried blossoms or flowers. Dredge the blossom in eggs and cream, followed by the flour and finally the bread crumbs. Place gently into the pan and fry until golden brown on both sides. Set on the cookie sheet to drain. Sprinkle with fresh lemon juice and serve.

Mafalda's Risotto alla Milanese

SERVES 8

⅔ *cup butter*
½ *onion, chopped*
½ *cup dry white wine*
5 *cups chicken broth*
1 *pound Arborio rice*
¼ *teaspoon saffron powder*
Salt and freshly ground black pepper to taste
1 *cup grated Parmigiano-Reggiano*

Melt ⅓ cup of the butter in a large pot, add the onion, and fry until it's golden. Add the wine and 7 tablespoons of the broth. Boil gently until reduced by about half.

Add the rice and cook for 5 minutes, stirring constantly. The mixture should be fairly dry in consistency. Add the saffron, salt, and pepper.

Continue cooking over low to medium heat for 20 minutes, stirring in the broth 1 cup at a time until the liquid is absorbed. The rice should remain tender throughout.

Remove from the stove and add the remaining ⅓ cup of butter and the cheese. Let stand for about a minute. Serve.

> *A Tip from Mary:* Mafalda always uses Arborio rice, as do most cooks in Lombardy, but there are other kinds of Italian varieties that work well. If you want to be authentic, try brands made in Italy.

> *A Tip from Adri:* I like to slice two portobello mushrooms and add them to the recipe above with the onion. Another alternative: I add a pound of medium shrimp. It's fun to experiment with different additions.

We would eat this risotto as a first course or as a side to a light meat supper—sometimes just *prosciutto* (only from Parma or San Daniele, which produce the best prosciutto) and a salad. Either way, Mafalda made it special, and, like all the cooks on this side of the Atlantic, she was at her happiest when she saw how much you enjoyed one of her meals.

THE BIG FINISH

CHAPTER SIX

Dessert, or Dessertina

For the Trigianis, the crowning glory of the meal was dessert. When Mom married Dad, she encountered an almost religious devotion to the concept of ending a meal with pastry, cake, or cookies. In the Bonicelli house, you had the occasional cookie or light cake, but it was by no means a nightly occurrence. Fresh fruit was Grandma Lucy's finale.

Before and after . . . cake.

So shortly after their wedding, after one of her first trips to the grocery store, Mom had to face an inquisition from Dad: Where are the cookies? Are you going to bake some? What kind? How about a pie? Mom's answer was that they had fruit for dessert. He was truly, deeply shocked.

We soon learned that if we helped Mom by making a dessert for dinner, we would win major points with Dad as well. That led to some really interesting experiments. Some might call them disasters.

✦ *Checka says:* "Adri attempted banana bread once and didn't take the time to mash the bananas—she just added them whole, right to the batter! It looked great until you cut a slice. Carlo took one look and asked Dad if he 'had' to eat it. The rest of us didn't even ask—we just ran."

✦ *Toni says:* "Then there was the time Adri iced a cake when it was still warm and then put those little silver sugar ball decorations on top. The decorations drowned in the icing as it sank into the cake, and no one knew they were in there. Dad broke a tooth, and those particular decorations were banned for all time."

Some experts believe that the growth of American baking traditions and dessert habits paralleled the increase of wealth in this country. The theory was, back at the beginning of the twentieth century, if you could afford sugar and flour and other expensive ingredients, it meant you had arrived. Whether this figured into Grandmom Trigiani's view of sweets, I don't know. But she loved to bake and she liked nothing better than seeing people compare portions: who got a center piece, who got a corner piece, who got a larger piece. While this was negative reinforcement, she took it as affirmation that her baked goods were in demand.

Grandmom Trigiani loved to bake on Sunday morning, after early Mass. She'd arrive home, change her clothes, and pull out her mother's slate pastry board, and the flour would fly. One of her favorite things to make, and one of the most popular, was the buttermilk cake, a Perin family standard. It became one of Pia's favorites as

well, and she made such a big fuss every time Grandmom made one that Grand-mom soon began baking them just for Pia. And if Grandmom was visiting us, she'd arrive with the cake wrapped first in plastic wrap, then a layer of aluminum foil. Checka loved it for the sugary topping, which she saved for last.

Perin Family Buttermilk Cake

SERVES 12

4 cups all-purpose flour
1 cup (2 sticks) unsalted butter, cut into small bits and softened (but still chilled)
1 teaspoon salt
2½ cups sugar
2 teaspoons baking powder
1 teaspoon baking soda
3 eggs
1 teaspoon vanilla extract
2 cups buttermilk

Preheat the oven to 350 degrees.

Place the flour, butter, and salt in a large bowl.

In a second bowl, mix the sugar, baking powder, and baking soda. Add this mixture to the flour mixture. Combine, then measure out 1 cup and set aside.

Beat the eggs, vanilla, and buttermilk into the mixture.

Pour the batter into a greased and floured 9 × 12-inch cake pan. Sprinkle the reserved cup of flour-sugar mixture over the top of the batter. Bake for 45 minutes to 1 hour, watching for the cake to turn a golden color.

Tipsy Lady from Flicksville Ice Box Cake

SERVES 10 TO 12 VERY HAPPY PARTY GUESTS

Grandmom Viola made this cake for special occasions. It was a birthday request cake, and often showed up as the finale of her most elegant dinner parties. This recipe will re-mind you of tiramisu, but it will also remind you of the great cream-filled American cakes served on those rolling carts in swanky hotels. Assemble in layers and by the end it will look like the Roman Colosseum in a truffle dish!

CAKE

3 packages of ladyfinger sponge cookies (or around 50 ladyfinger cookies; to bake your own, see page 124)

½ cup amaretto liqueur (applied with a baker's brush)

FILLING

8 ounces Baker's semi-sweet chocolate

4 tablespoons boiling water

6 eggs, separated

3 tablespoons powdered sugar

2 teaspoons vanilla

TOPPING

2 cups heavy cream

4 tablespoons confectioners' sugar

1 teaspoon vanilla extract

If you have a deep crystal bowl or a trifle bowl or a clear or rectangular dessert dish (8 ×11), all work for the presentation of this cake. However, Gram made it in a deep, clear trifle bowl, which, when served, looked elegant.

Line the bottom and sides of the serving dish with the ladyfingers. Have fun—create a pattern on the base of the dish and line the sides up to the edge. Brush the ladyfingers with the amaretto evenly until it soaks in. Cover and place in the refrigerator as you prep the filling and topping. Set aside the remaining ladyfingers to create the layers.

Melt the chocolate with 4 tablespoons boiling water over very low heat. Cool a bit, then beat in the 6 egg yolks, one at a time. Add the sugar and vanilla; stir thoroughly until dissolved. Beat the egg whites and fold them in (they should be creamy). The chocolate cream should be the consistency of frosting.

You are now ready to create the cake layers. Remove the ladyfingers drenched in liqueur from the refrigerator. Add a layer of the chocolate cream, then a layer of the ladyfingers, and alternate chocolate cream and ladyfingers until you reach the top of the dish. Cover tightly and refrigerate overnight.

To make the whipped cream topping: Pour the cream into a bowl and add the sugar and vanilla. Using an electric hand mixer or balloon whisk, beat the cream until it is dense. Add more confectioners' sugar to thicken the whipped cream. Before serving, remove from the refrigerator. Serve the cake with a dollop of fresh cream.

Ladyfingers

Viola's Ice Box Cake can surely be constructed with packaged ladyfingers, but there's nothing like the real cookie, delicate, golden, and sweet.

2 tablespoons of butter (to grease pan)
2 whole eggs
6 eggs separated
2 teaspoons vanilla extract
½ cup granulated sugar
1 cup cake flour, sifted
powdered sugar (to dust)

Preheat the oven to 350. Grease your baking sheet lightly with butter. Set aside.

Combine eggs, separated egg yolks, vanilla, and sugar until well blended. Whisk the flour into the egg mixture. Set aside.

Whip the egg whites into soft clouds. Add about half the whipped egg whites into your mixture, whipping gently, until well blended, then add the rest of the egg whites, whipping until batter is light and airy, yet is not runny and has some heft. It it's runny, whisk more flour into the batter. (I've found eggs cause a variance!) Load this batter into a pastry bag.

Press the batter on the buttered baking sheet into 3- to 4-inch strips. The cookies should be about 1 inch wide pre-baked. Leave about ½ inch between each ladyfinger on the baking sheet. Bake about 15 minutes until golden.

Sometimes you will have to flip the pan in the oven to bake the ladyfingers evenly. Gently remove. When cooked, dust lightly with powdered sugar. This recipe yields about 72 ladyfingers, which is plenty as a component for the Tipsy Lady from Flicksville Ice Box Cake.

Grandma Lucy's hard little cookies, *pezzi duri* (literally, "hard pieces"), a form of what we know as biscotti, are perfect for dunking in espresso.

Grandma Lucy's Pezzi Duri

MAKES ABOUT 3 DOZEN

6 eggs
¾ cup sugar
½ cup vegetable oil
½ pound sliced blanched almonds
Dash of salt
1½ teaspoons baking powder
½ teaspoon anise seed
1 teaspoon anise extract
1 cup all-purpose flour

Separate the eggs. In a large bowl, beat the yolks. Keep the whites to the side; take about a tablespoonful out and place it in a separate bowl.

Combine the beaten yolks with the sugar, oil, almonds, salt, baking powder, anise seed, and anise extract. Add the egg whites and mix well.

Preheat the oven to 375 degrees.

Roll the mixture into 4 long (27-inch) rolls. Add flour as necessary to bind the rolls and hold their shape. Place them on a cookie sheet, about 1 inch apart.

Place the cookie sheet in the oven and bake for 20 minutes.

Remove the sheet from the oven and brush the rolls with the reserved egg white. Cut the rolls into 3-inch strips.

Another favorite that we've discovered many Italian families enjoy was called *crostoli* by Grandma Lucy. These little pastries dusted in sugar melt in your mouth. It was one of the few recipes that crossed the Bonicelli border into Trigiani Land. Grandmom Trigiani became adept at making them as well. Viola was no laggard when it came to incorporating a great cookie into her dessert arsenal.

Crostoli

MAKES 2 TO 3 DOZEN PASTRIES, DEPENDING ON THE SIZE OF THE PIECES

4 extra-large eggs
5 tablespoons granulated sugar

2 cups all-purpose flour
3 tablespoons baking powder
½ teaspoon salt
2 to 3 cups vegetable oil
Confectioners' sugar, for sprinkling

In a large bowl, beat the eggs with the granulated sugar. Add the flour, baking powder, and salt, mixing well.

Begin heating the oil in a saucepan over high heat until it is ready for frying the dough. (Take a small, test piece of the dough and drop it in the oil. If the dough rises to the surface, the oil is ready.)

Roll the dough into a thin layer using a pastry roller. Then, using a pizza cutter with a serrated edge, cut the dough into various lengths. Tie each length of dough into a loose knot and drop the prepared dough into the hot oil piece by piece. There should only be a few of the prepared pastries frying at a time. Remove the pastries once they have fried to a golden hue. Place them on paper towels to absorb the excess oil. Sprinkle with the confectioners' sugar and serve on a pretty plate. They especially look nice when stacked high.

Grandmom Trigiani was always experimenting, and her miniature cupcakes were such a hit the first time she made them, they are now a family classic. They arrived on the scene in the seventies. They're not traditionally Italian, but they evoke the rich desserts that use mascarpone cheese.

Miniature Cupcakes
MAKES 7 TO 8 DOZEN

FILLING
8 ounces cream cheese
1 egg
⅓ cup sugar
⅛ teaspoon salt

In a medium bowl, beat all ingredients until creamy.

CAKE BATTER

1½ cups all-purpose flour

¼ cup cocoa

1 cup sugar

1 teaspoon baking soda

½ teaspoon salt

1 cup water

½ cup vegetable oil

1 tablespoon white vinegar

½ teaspoon vanilla extract

TOPPING

6 ounces miniature bittersweet chocolate chips

Preheat the oven to 350 degrees.

In a large mixing bowl, combine the flour, cocoa, sugar, baking soda, and salt.

In a separate bowl, combine the water, oil, vinegar, and vanilla. Add to the dry ingredients and mix.

Using miniature cupcake tins lined with paper wrappers, fill each cup half full with the batter. Then drop in ½ teaspoon of the filling. Finally, drop a couple of miniature chocolate chips on top. Bake for 20 minutes. Remove from the oven and allow to cool, then store in the refrigerator.

Grandmom Trigiani also liked to make rolled pastries, and this one seems Middle Eastern or even Eastern European in origin. I guess some version of this wonderful pastry is found in nearly every cuisine. Grandmom made two versions, and she probably picked up this recipe at a cocktail party.

Nut or Poppy Seed Rolls
MAKES 4 LOAVES

PASTRY

2 packets of active dry yeast

1¼ cups warm milk

4 tablespoons sugar

¼ *pound (1 stick) unsalted butter*
4½ *cups all-purpose flour*
2 *egg yolks, beaten*
1 *teaspoon salt*

Place the yeast in a pan and add the warm milk and sugar. Let stand while you combine the butter and flour, as if for a pie crust, in a large bowl. Make a well in the center of the butter-flour mixture and place the egg yolks, salt, and yeast mixture there. Mix until smooth and the dough leaves the side of the bowl easily.

Divide the dough into 4 parts and roll out to about ¼ inch thick. Spread with the filling. Roll.

Place each filled roll in a greased 15 × 10-inch jelly-roll pan, cover with a cloth, and let stand in a warm place for about an hour. Preheat the oven to 350 degrees.

Bake the rolls uncovered for 30 to 45 minutes, just until brown. Remove from the oven and cover with a damp cloth immediately; keep covered for 10 minutes. Slice into pieces 1 inch in width.

NUT FILLING

½ *pound almonds, ground*
⅛ *pound (½ stick) unsalted butter*
½ *teaspoon vanilla extract*
¾ *cup honey*
⅓ *cup brown sugar*

Combine the ingredients in a medium saucepan and cook over low heat until the butter melts. Mix well and allow to cool.

POPPY SEED FILLING

½ *pound ground poppy seeds*
¼ *cup corn syrup*
½ *cup sugar*
⅛ *pound (½ stick) unsalted butter*

Combine the ingredients in a medium saucepan and cook over low heat, stirring constantly, until it boils. Remove from the heat immediately; allow to cool.

Saint Joseph's Day celebration featuring nut- and poppyseed-filled delicacies.

Cookie platters were a part of every special day in Roseto: milestone birthdays, baptisms, weddings, First Communions, even funerals. They were as elaborate as the living rooms embellished with crystal, velvet, brocade, and marble that came to represent success in the new country. And they were as festooned as the outfits you'd see on the Roseto women for any of these events. (Except a funeral—plain black, of course.)

The most high-profile cookie platter venue was, hands-down, the Roseto wedding. This event always featured a wedding cake, but the long tables bore round platters of gorgeous cookies, made by the women of the town and shared with the bride's family. There was one special cookie that was like a small cake itself, not like an American cupcake, but denser and smaller, in the shape of a dome. (The ornament you see in the photograph on page 133 adorned Grandmom and Grandpop Trigiani's wedding cake in 1932.) As wedding parties got bigger, with bridesmaids in elaborate get-ups, it became a common practice to ice these cookies in the colors of the bridesmaids' gowns. Some of the cookies were iced white and dusted with coconut, in honor of the bride.

Auguri!

Wedding Cookies

MAKES 3 DOZEN

PASTRY

¼ pound (1 stick) unsalted butter

¼ pound (1 stick) unsalted margarine

1 cup sugar

3 large eggs

1 teaspoon almond extract

½ cup milk

3¼ to 3½ cups all-purpose flour

Pinch of salt

5 teaspoons baking powder

Preheat the oven to 350 degrees.

In a large bowl, cream the butter, margarine, sugar, and eggs together. Then add the almond extract, milk, flour, salt, and baking powder.

Keeping your hands wet, shape a piece of dough into a ball (baci-style— a little higher in the middle). Bake on an ungreased baking sheet for 13 minutes, or until lightly brown.

Cool.

ICING

½ pound (½ box) confectioners' sugar

2 tablespoons butter

1 tablespoon milk, plus more if needed

Almond flavoring to taste

Food coloring, if desired

Shredded sweetened coconut, for dipping

Mix all ingredients but coconut together until a frosting consistency is reached. Ice the cooled cookies and dip into shredded coconut.

> *A Tip from Toni:* After icing, arrange these on a dish and cover tightly with plastic wrap. These cookies can get a little hard when left in the air.

Match the wedding cookies and the bridesmaid gowns!

This punch recipe comes by way of one of my Big Stone Gap friends who came from a temperate family, so I had to make the run to the ABC store for the liquor fixins' for this punch. These days, you can get the champagne at the grocery store, but you still have to go to the ABC store for the brandy and Curaçao. There was always a non-alcohol punch served at the wedding receptions, but the Drunk on Love punch always won the popularity contest.

Drunk on Love Wedding Punch
SERVES 14 TO 16

One 46-ounce can pineapple rings
One 8-ounce jar maraschino cherries
1 cup granulated sugar
½ cup lemon juice
½ cup water
3 ounces brandy
3 ounces Curaçao
3 ounces maraschino juice
1 well-chilled bottle (1 liter) sparkling water
3 well-chilled bottles champagne (750 ml)
1 bottle (1 liter) lemon-lime soda
Sprigs of fresh mint

At the bottom of a pretty punch bowl, place pineapple rings. In the center of the rings place a maraschino cherry. Make the design up the sides of the bowl; it will make it look pretty on the table. In a separate large bowl, dissolve the sugar in the lemon juice and water. Slowly pour in the brandy, Curaçao, and maraschino juice, mixing well. Pour in the chilled sparkling water, champagne, and soda, and stir. Garnish with sprigs of fresh mint.

Personal style signified another cultural awakening when the Bonicellis merged with the Trigianis. As a seamstress and the default alterations expert in Chisholm, Grandma Lucy was renowned for the beauty of her stitching, so much so that if you turn the hem of one of her pieces, you marvel at the even spacing and straight rows. (She and her craftsmanship were the inspiration for the main character in my

Dad and Mom at the Morris Inn, Notre Dame, Indiana, as they dive into their reception feast. They were married on a Monday. Mom is refreshingly unconventional.

novel *Lucia, Lucia,* and not just because of her beautiful name!) Grandma Lucy made the majority of her twin daughters' clothes until they were well into their married lives. This included work clothes, wedding dresses and trousseaus, maternity clothes, and evening dresses. Mary still wears a two-piece black peau-de-soie evening outfit that Grandma Lucy made for Mom forty-odd years ago. The elegance and richness of these clothes come not from over-the-top design but from tailoring and quality fabrics. Think Jacqueline Kennedy, not Gina Lollobrigida.

When Mrs. Kennedy became famous for the pillbox hat, Mom was a little affronted, because she'd been wearing them for years. In fact, her wedding veil, circa 1956, was attached to a narrow pillbox that Mom had made herself. It was so classic that when Checka married Tom Noone in 1999, she wore the same veil.

Mom loved to make hats. When she dresses for church on Sunday, Mom wears a hat. She isn't a feather and flower type, unless it is a single embellishment. Mom must have a beret in every color of the universe. When we were little, Mom made sure her daughters had all the equipment as well. We wore hats, gloves, dress shoes, and feminine frocks.

> ✦ *Mary says:* "Adri bristled at all the accessories and was always scratching and pulling at her clothes. Mom could count on having to search for little white gloves in between the seats after Adri got out of the car. That, and she always had to straighten her hat and pull up her socks."

Mary's First Holy Communion is the perfect example of Mom's fashion ethic.

A child's First Holy Communion is a special day in the life of Roman Catholics, and Mary's day was made even more special by the presence of Don Andrea. A journalist as well as a priest, our great-uncle had chosen to remain at home in Bergamo and run the newspaper there rather than accept a post in Rome when Cardinal Angelo Roncalli was elected pope. John XXIII was from Bergamo, and over the years, the two had come to know each other well. This minimal degree of separation from the Holy Father was viewed gratefully and with all the appropriate reverence. When Mom and Dad heard that Don Andrea would be visiting the United States at the time of Mary's First Communion, they naturally informed Father Gennaro Leone, the pastor of Roseto's church. Father Leone invited Don Andrea to concelebrate the Mass.

Well, the only thing bigger would have been if the pope were coming himself. At home, Mary was coached for days about how, in addition to preparing herself for the privilege of the sacrament of Holy Communion, she had to be a perfect example of Catholic girlhood. At school, the Salesian sisters were all over the entire class to ensure the same.

Mom had very specific plans for Mary's ensemble. And they diverged from the typical Roseto outfit for a little girl's First Communion. All the other girls in the class would be done up in frothy confections of white lace and tulle—including foofy skirts, short sleeves, and even foofier veils attached to elaborate crowns or headpieces, all of which mimicked the look of the typical Roseto bride. Mary soon learned that she would be the lone Givenchy/Cassini/Valentino-inspired communicant. Grandma

Mary's First Holy Communion with Don Andrea.

Lucy made her dress, a straight chemise of white satin that buttoned up the back and had long sleeves. The only embellishments were the tiny pearl buttons. And the veil was a mini-Mom, made by her: pillbox hat with veil straight down the back.

◆*Mary says:* "Elegant, and, in retrospect, entirely appropriate. If I walk down the aisle in a white dress again (whatever the reason), I hope it's in the same sophisticated motif. Except for the headgear. Mom had my hair pulled back in the tightest ponytail of my seven-year-old existence, and there must have been four hat pins in addition to the elastic band holding that veil in place. Besides being my First Communion, it was my First Headache."

Nothing gets in the way of Mom's sense of propriety or taste. She is steadfast in her sensibilities, which have influenced each of her daughters in only the best way. In the kitchen, on the job, at the party. Italians call this dedication to dressing with impact "*fare una bella figura*," which loosely translated means to cut a fine figure. The women in our family have great style, yet style has meant something different for each one. And they all have shared the obsession with *la bella figura* at the table as well.

Those Roseto cookie platters were true works of art. In Grandmom Trigiani's kitchen and on her platters you would find sno balls, fishes, and *taralli*. The latter are a southern Italian treat made two ways, sweet and savory, often served with wine.

Sno Balls

MAKES 3 DOZEN

½ pound (2 sticks) unsalted butter, softened
6 tablespoons sugar
2 cups all-purpose flour
1 teaspoon vanilla extract
1 cup ground pecans
¼ cup confectioners' sugar

Preheat the oven to 300 degrees.

Combine the ingredients except the confectioners' sugar in a bowl. To make the cookies, take a teaspoonful at a time and roll into a ball. Place on a greased cookie sheet, about 2 inches apart.

Bake for 30 minutes. Let cool a bit, but roll in the confectioners' sugar while they're still a little warm.

The Fountains of Rome Summer Fruit Compote

SERVES 6 TO 8

1 orange
1 lemon
½ cup light brown sugar
¼ tsp ground nutmeg
6 ripe apricots

1 fresh pineapple, diced into chunks

6 ripe peaches, quartered (with skins)

2 cups pitted black cherries

4 tablespoons unsalted butter

1 pint fresh mascarpone cheese

Preheat the oven to 350 degrees.

Grate the rind from the lemon and orange, mix with the light brown sugar and nutmeg, and stir. Set aside. Cut remaining orange and lemon thin, combine with the apricots, pineapple, peaches, and cherries, and stir well. Add half of the lemon, orange, brown sugar, and nutmeg mixture in with the fruit; stir well. Place the fruit in a large casserole dish and pat with butter (about half a stick of butter sliced thin). Sprinkle the remaining lemon and orange zest and sugar and nutmeg mix on top. Bake for 30 minutes until bubbly. Serve with a dollop of fresh mascarpone cheese on top.

Fishes

MAKES ABOUT 3 DOZEN

FILLING

6 egg whites

½ pound crushed walnuts

½ pound confectioners' sugar

DOUGH

6 egg yolks

½ pound (2 sticks) unsalted butter, softened

2 cups all-purpose flour

In a medium bowl, mix the ingredients for the filling and set aside. Preheat the oven to 350 degrees.

In a large bowl, mix the dough ingredients together until smooth. Roll out into a piece about 2 × 12 inches long and 1 inch thick. Spread with filling—not too full—and roll closed. Cut into pieces about 2½ inches long and form into a crescent, closing both ends by pinching. Bake 8 to 12 minutes, or until lightly brown.

Taralli

Sweet Taralli

MAKES 2 DOZEN

4 eggs
⅓ cup granulated sugar
1 teaspoon ground cinnamon
2 tablespoons anisette
½ teaspoon vanilla extract
3½ cups all-purpose flour
¼ cup olive oil

In a large bowl, beat 3 of the eggs with the sugar. Add the cinnamon, anisette, vanilla extract, and flour to form a dough. Cover and set aside in a cool place for 2 hours.

Take a piece of the dough and roll it between your hands, making a pencil-like shape 4 to 5 inches long. Create a circle by joining the ends together and pinching them closed. Beat the remaining egg and brush each piece.

In a small saucepan, heat the olive oil, which should be about ¾ inch deep. Fry the rings three at a time until brown. Remove and drain on paper towels.

Savory Taralli

MAKES 4 DOZEN

½ packet (1¼ teaspoons) active dry yeast
½ cup lukewarm water (105–110 degrees)
¾ cup vegetable oil
2 eggs, lightly beaten
1 teaspoon salt
1 tablespoon fennel seed
4 cups all-purpose flour

In a large bowl, dissolve the yeast in the lukewarm water and allow to bubble. Add the rest of the ingredients, except the flour, to the yeast mixture. Add the flour and mix well.

Preheat the oven to 350 degrees.

Take a piece of the dough and roll it between your hands, making a pencil-like shape 4 to 5 inches long. Create a circle by joining the ends together and pinching them closed. Place on a greased cookie sheet and bake for about 8 minutes, or until lightly brown.

Cool.

Dogwood Garden Club Mimosa

SERVES 8

To my knowledge, I grew up in a dry county (minus our basement wine cellar and dad's bar and the ABC store in downtown Big Stone Gap). Mimosa trees were beautiful in the spring in the Appalachians, so we named this one in honor of Mom's garden club. Please forgive us, teetotalers, and to the rest, bottoms up!

8 fresh raspberries, washed
1 cup fresh squeezed orange juice
1 bottle of champagne
½ cup Grand Marnier liqueur

Line up 8 champagne flutes. Drop a raspberry in the base of each flute. Fill each flute one-quarter full with fresh squeezed orange juice. Top off with champagne until each flute is three-quarters full, then splash each flute with 1 tablespoon of Grand Marnier liqueur.

Pair with Savory Taralli.

Viola and Mary's Hawaiian Adventure Bars

MAKES 3 DOZEN SMALL BARS

Grandmom and her sister-in-law Mary Farino took a trip to Hawaii together in 1974. One of their favorite stops on the trip was a tour of the pineapple factory, which inspired much baking and cooking with pineapples when they returned to the mainland. Here's one of their pineapple treats.

1 cup sifted all-purpose flour
½ teaspoon baking soda

Viola with a friend in Honolulu.

COOKING WITH MY SISTERS

½ teaspoon salt

⅔ cup brown sugar

1 tablespoon brown sugar (set aside for topping)

⅔ cup drained, crushed pineapple

1 cup rolled oats

½ cup shortening

1 can pineapple rings

4 maraschino cherries, halved

Preheat the oven to 350 degrees. Sift together the dry ingredients. In a separate bowl, combine the crushed pineapple, oats, and shortening. Stir in the dry ingredients until well blended. Pat about half the mixture into a 9-inch square pan on the bottom evenly. Add the rings of pineapple on top of the first layer of the mixture. Take the remaining mixture and pat on top of the pineapple circles. Save two pineapple circles for the top. Slice one edge and twist into a bow shape, placing a maraschino cherry on either side. Do the same with the second pineapple ring. Sprinkle pineapple "ribbons" with brown sugar. Bake for 25 to 30 minutes.

For a little more drama in a dinner-party setting, there was always the zabaglione. We attribute Dad's lifelong love affair with dessert—his pet name for the course was "dessertina"—to the fresh zabaglione he had every morning as a child. This recipe, though, is Grandma Lucy's. After Grandpa Carlo became ill, she made this for him every day.

✦ *Mom says:* "This not only tastes good, it's nutritious. There were many days when it was difficult for Papa to eat. But Mama would make him the zabaglione, and sometimes he would even pour a little red wine in it."

Zabaglione

SERVES 4

5 egg yolks
1 whole egg
2 tablespoons sugar
½ cup Marsala wine

In the top of a double boiler, place the egg yolks, whole egg, and sugar. Set over a simmering pot of water. Beat, by hand, with a wire whisk until the mixture is yellow and frothy.

Gradually blend in the Marsala a small amount at a time. Continue using the whisk, over the simmering water, until the mixture increases in volume. This should take no more than 10 minutes.

When the mixture holds its shape on a spoon, it is ready to serve. Serve warm in dessert bowls or in stemware.

Dad would often recall how special he was made to feel by his morning zabaglione, and he used the story to remind us of the honored role of the first-born son. Of course, Dad's aunts used to mutter "spoiled" under their breaths, but they were just as guilty of the ancient Italian practice of elevating sons above daughters. Even Grandma Lucy would beam when her Orlando entered the room. For these women, their sons were knights in shining armor. In Lucy's case, Orlando was the only man in an all-female household, yet he was respectful of women and a true gentleman. She taught him well.

And Grandmom Trigiani, well, logic and sentiment did win occasionally, particularly when her granddaughters had made their way in the world and would return to dote on her and learn from her. Ultimately, Viola realized that because of her own tendencies and by her own design, and as much as some of her grandsons would spend time with her in the kitchen, that room was the province of women. By the end of her life, she would say often that her granddaughters brought her comfort and humor, a surprise to her but a reward for us.

Aloha from Ida the photographer in Honolulu.

The Big Wow

CHAPTER SEVEN

Snacks and Treats

The concept that a person had access to food only three times a day, at regularly scheduled meals, was as foreign to us as the Trigianis were to Big Stone Gap. We probably got our snacking gene from Dad's side, although Mom would shudder at the thought that anyone was hungry. She made sure we had plenty of healthy snacks around. This chapter, though, is largely about the special touches we might find hiding in Grandmom Trigiani's kitchen, or just coming out of her oven.

But first, a word about Grandma Lucy's eating philosophy.

She used to say that all one really needed at a meal was a fist-size portion of food. (And she never met a health club physical trainer, diet doctor, or fitness guru.) But she ate when she was hungry. And she generally reached for a piece of fruit or a few nuts. Mom would let us eat a small snack when we got home from school in the afternoon, but she monitored our intake because she didn't want dinner ruined. Same treatment for Dad; if he came home and she noticed his head in the refrigerator one too many times, she'd remind him how much she was working to make him a nice dinner. Guilt was always a good incentive in Ida's kitchen.

♦ *Toni says:* "Yes, but it rarely worked on Dad. I first tasted Gorgonzola thanks to one of Dad's before-dinner snacks. Not only was his head in the refrigerator, he always found the primo stuff."

From the Trigianis we learned that there were more than fifty ways to classify your snack. So we were pretty inventive. Mary remembers the boys, in particular, concocting mini-meals. A favorite of ours was to toast sliced bread, spread mayonnaise on it, and throw lettuce in the middle. One of those got you through your midafternoon slump. I liked anything with vinegar on it. We all liked radishes and carrots, too. Grandma Lucy used to keep a supply of radishes in cold water in the sink at the back of her shoe shop. And Mom had a great recipe for pickled eggs. The amount of vinegar needed depends on the size of the eggs and the size of the container.

Pickled Eggs

MAKES 1 DOZEN

1 dozen hard-boiled eggs
One 16-ounce can round beets with juice
White vinegar
1 tablespoon whole peppercorns

Place the eggs into a ½- to 1-gallon glass container. Add the beets with their juice. Completely fill the jar with vinegar. Sprinkle the peppercorns on the top and seal.

Refrigerate for at least 24 hours. The longer the eggs are allowed to cure, the darker the color will become and the stronger the beet-vinegar flavoring will be in the eggs.

Loving restaurants the way Dad did, we logged a lot of time in some nice establishments. We also learned early on from Dad how to order. For example, if we were in a seafood restaurant and someone ordered a hamburger, Dad would make a huge point about how one should always have fish in a seafood restaurant—both because it was what they did best and because you should try everything. He wanted us to experience everything we could, which is why even a humble snack got the *all'italiana* treatment.

Dad would always look at a plate first and admire it, even if it was a lowly sandwich. Although when it came to Grandmom Trigiani, no sandwich was lowly. It was actually a meal. And if you were lucky enough to be with Viola on a car trip, her handbag was a bottomless treasure chest of snacks. Sometimes she would pack an entire grocery bag of snacks, and invariably the packer of the car, usually Dad, would complain about there not being enough room for another piece of luggage, and proclaim we'd just stop on the road. Then, Grandmom would complain about the cost of said side trip, both in terms of dollars and time. Two hours into the trip and too early for a stop, someone would say he or she was hungry, and Grandmom would utter her legendary words, "Mmph, I thought you didn't want my sandwiches!"

✦ *Toni says:* "On one trip back to Big Stone Gap, in the middle of a winter storm, we got caught in a huge traffic jam. We made it through the two-hour-plus wait because Grandmom had snuck a bag of sandwiches and cookies into the car when Dad wasn't looking. After that, Dad never complained about Grandmom's bags!"

When she was in her eighties, Grandmom Trigiani would take the bus with her friends to Atlantic City, and she always packed a bag then, too, even though one of the biggest incentives for these groups was the free meal they got at the casino.

Chewing on a toothpick, Grandmom serves turkey.

Viola Trigiani: "I'm so sick of *slots*." Grandmom, who loved gambling as much as cooking, finally admits she's tired of the emotional roller coaster of winning and losing in Atlantic City.

Dear Adri:
How are you?
We miss you around here. Toni and I had a nice time in Aruba. Today I'm off to A.C. I'm so sick of *slots*. Picked up this little hair dohickey in Aruba. Have a Happy Birthday. I'm late so forgive me.
Love Grandmom.

Grandmom's Ham and Butter Sandwiches

4 ounces (1 stick) sweet cream butter, or fresh if you can find it
1 loaf of Italian bread, preferably on the sweet side, cut into 8 pieces of equal width
1 pound ham, preferably Italian prosciutto, cut into very thin slices

Spread the butter on both sides of the bread and layer on the ham. Now you have sandwiches!

One of our favorite road snacks was the ham and butter sandwich. While Grandmom Trigiani generally preferred more Italian-style ham, she was an equal-opportunity ham buyer. And, she always had ham, in some variety, in her refrigerator. One could never go hungry if there was ham, bread, and butter in the house. Which brings us to The Virginia Ham Story.

Grandmom not only had a second kitchen in the basement, she had an extra refrigerator in the garage. So when she and Grandpop bought a ham on their way back from one of their visits to Big Stone Gap, she put it in the garage refrigerator.

Grandpop had a handsome German shepherd named Duke who lived in a pen outside the house. When Grandpop let him out of the pen, Duke would go bananas trying to play with us, run, search for small animals, run in circles, try to get in the house, and did I mention, run? At about twenty miles per hour. When Grandpop was going to let Duke out of his pen, he would give us the high sign, and those of us who weren't up for Duke's antics would take cover.

One Saturday afternoon, Grandmom decided to clean the garage refrigerator. The contents of the refrigerator were placed gently on a clean towel on the floor of the garage, except for the Virginia ham, which she carried into the kitchen and left on the counter. She kept the door open to the kitchen so she could move back and forth between it and the garage. At the same time, and unbeknownst to her, Grandpop headed out to Duke's pen to let him out. You can guess the rest. Within thirty seconds of receiving his freedom, and this is not an exaggeration, Duke's food radar pulled him right into the kitchen and right to that ham. It was gone in another thirty seconds.

Grandmom was apoplectic. This was on the level of a tragedy for her. So what

From left: Adri, Michael, Mary, Toni, and Pia. No matter how casual the occasion, Pia always wore black patent-leather Mary Janes.

ensued was one of the biggest, most entertaining arguments we had witnessed to date. Meanwhile, Duke was the calmest we had ever seen him, his belly full, too tired to chase us for sport.

Less than a year later, Grandpop would be gone. Duke died a few days before Grandpop, but Grandmom decided to spare him the news. Cooking, baking, and tending her gardens took on even more importance after Grandpop's death. She mourned her husband for a very long time, and working in the kitchen kept her busy. Like Grandma Lucy, Grandmom Trigiani never remarried. We still spent our summers at Camp Viola, but it wasn't the same. We missed Grandpop. Our rewards for the free labor were a dip in the pool and some really great snacks.

✦ *Pia says:* "I remember the afternoons with pizze fritte. This was a treat not only because it was tasty but because it required standing over a hot pan or fryer of boiling fat. For Grandmom to do this in the middle of a summer day meant a special effort."

Most of the time, you got your annual fix of *pizze fritte* (also called *zeppole* in some parts of Italy) at the Big Time, the week-long event associated with the Roseto parish's celebration of its patron, Our Lady of Mount Carmel. There was always a carnival with various food stands, and the most popular was the Sodality's booth, where battalions of women made the specialty. The Sodality was a social organization for women of the church.

During the Big Time, they would work over the deep-fat fryers to prepare the pizze fritte for sale. They would chatter, try to fix up their children with appropriate matches, watch the crowd, and comment on the various outfits parading past them. Spontaneously, one of the ladies would start to sing, maybe one of the beautiful hymns to Mary or a traditional Italian song. Soon, everyone would join in. The women were fascinating to watch, their hands pressing the little bundles of dough into flat discs that would turn gold in the oil and then be removed, doused in sugar, and served to you in a little napkin. And the Sodality members were fascinating to hear, because in their conversation you caught the cadence of the old country.

Pizze Fritte (Fried Dough)

This is the same recipe as for Basic Pizza Dough, except that vegetable oil is used instead of olive oil.

MAKES 2 DOZEN PIECES

1 tablespoon active dry yeast
¾ cup warm water
Pinch of sugar
2½ cups unbleached all-purpose flour
3 tablespoons vegetable oil
1 teaspoon salt
3 cups shortening or vegetable oil
1 cup granulated or confectioners' sugar

In a small mixing bowl, dissolve the yeast in the warm water with the sugar. Set aside for 5 minutes.

On a large, flat surface, pour the flour into a mound, shaping a large well in the center. Pour the yeast mixture, 1 tablespoon of the vegetable oil, and the salt into the well. Then slowly work the flour into the center, using your fingers. Begin forming the mixture into a ball, kneading it until the dough can stretch. This takes between 10 and 15 minutes. Keep a little warm water close by, using a little at a time in case you need it to work the dough. The dough should always be soft but not wet.

Place the ball of dough into a large mixing bowl that you've coated lightly with vegetable oil. Turn the ball over until it's covered with the oil. Then cover the bowl with a clean dish towel. Put the dough in a warm place, away from any drafts, to rise. In about an hour and a half, it should be double its original size. At that point, it's ready.

Heat the shortening or remaining oil in a deep-fryer or large sauce pot. Using a knife, cut the dough into 2 × 4-inch pieces, and stretch them out with your fingertips. Drop a few pieces of dough into the hot oil and brown them for a short time, turning once; they should be light brown in color. Remove and drain on paper towels. While still warm, sprinkle with the sugar, and serve.

> *A Tip from Pia:* Experiment with making this a savory snack. Grandmom would make appetizers by forming smaller pieces of dough and stuffing them with anchovies, roasted peppers, mozzarella, or canned banana peppers before frying them.

> *A Tip from Checka:* Use frozen bread dough or purchase fresh dough from a local bakery.

Grandmom Trigiani always kept a couple of canned specialties on hand, including golden banana peppers stuffed with anchovies. Sometimes they were spicy hot; you had to check the handwritten label on the jar to make sure. Otherwise, you were the entertainment, depending on the scale of the heat and the intensity of your reaction. These are delicious, though, especially with Italian or French bread.

Canned Peppers Stuffed with Anchovies

SERVES 6

1 quart pepperoncini (finger-shaped) green peppers, pickled in vinegar—hot or mild
4 ounces anchovy fillets
⅓ cup olive oil

Slice the peppers lengthwise, one side only, and remove the seeds. Insert an anchovy fillet or two.

Arrange the peppers in a serving dish and coat with the olive oil. Cover and allow to marinate for at least 2 hours before serving.

Serve with Italian bread.

Crostini Yolanda

SERVES 8 TO 10

I've missed my grandmother Viola's canned banana peppers with alige (anchovy) in vinegar and olive oil every summer since she passed on. We intend to can her signature pepper eventually, and hopefully, this will be the summer we attempt to bring back the glory. In the meantime, this recipe is as close as you can get to the experience of her beloved creation, which I ramped up with a fresh ricotta spread. She would say, "What a dish!"

1 long baguette (a classic two-footer), sliced thin in rounds

TOPPING
3 yellow peppers, chopped fine
3 red peppers, chopped fine
3 anchovy fillets, chopped fine
1 tablespoon olive oil

RICOTTA SPREAD

2 cups fresh ricotta
1 tablespoon fresh mint
1 lemon, grated for zest (save juice)

Preheat the oven to 300 degrees. Slice the baguette into thin rounds, place on a cookie sheet, drizzle with olive oil, lightly toast, and remove from oven. Set aside.

Mix the yellow and red peppers with the anchovy fillets and olive oil in a bowl until well blended.

To make ricotta spread: whisk the fresh ricotta, fresh mint, and lemon zest, until creamy. Squeeze lemon juice over the mixture, and stir thoroughly.

Dollop the ricotta spread onto the bread slices. Create a small well in the ricotta, and fill with the pepper and anchovy topping. Garnish with a mint sprig and serve.

Excellent when paired with Pennsylvania birch beer (non-alcoholic) or the real thing.

Lavinia's Strawberry Bellini
SERVES 6 IN CHAMPAGNE FLUTES

We named this Bellini after our grandmother Viola's baby sister, who was to meet her eldest sister at dawn to pick strawberries at a farm early one summer morning in 1990. Lavinia arrived ahead of the sun and waited for the farm truck to take her to the field. As the sun was rising, the truck drove over the hill. She could see someone on the back of the truck, legs dangling. As the truck came closer, Lavinia realized it was Viola, surrounded by baskets of plump, red, freshly picked strawberries. "You're late," Viola said to Lavinia. Here's a Bellini for "Ziwinnia," who after that, could've used a drink.

¼ cup sugar
3 tablespoons water
4 cups chilled fresh strawberries
6 fresh strawberries, deleafed (set aside)
2 tablespoons fresh lemon juice
1 bottle Prosecco

Boil the sugar and water to make a simple syrup. In a blender, blend the strawberries and lemon juice; strain. Add the syrup to the strawberry mixture. Add Prosecco and stir. Drop one fresh strawberry into each champagne flute and pour the mixture equally into each of the six flutes.

Pair with Crostini Yolanda.

As I've said, a lot of Grandmom Trigiani's dishes were treated like gold and parceled out as such. One of them was the potato pizza, which is actually a small loaf of bread. If you are a potato person, this snack is for you.

Potato Pizza
MAKES 3 LOAVES

DOUGH
1 packet active dry yeast
1 cup warm water
2½ cups all-purpose flour
1 teaspoon salt
1 tablespoon olive oil

Dissolve the yeast in ¼ cup of the warm water and set aside until bubbly.

Combine the flour and the salt and place on a cutting board, forming a well in the center. Add the yeast mixture, the remaining ¾ cup of water, and the olive oil and slowly mix in the flour. Keep mixing until all the flour has been added and continue to mix by hand. Knead until the dough is soft and elastic. Place in a bowl and rub with olive oil. Cover and let rise.

When the dough has risen to about double the original size, knead again. Divide the dough into 3 even pieces.

FILLING
4 medium potatoes
1 large sweet onion
¼ cup olive oil
Salt and freshly ground black pepper to taste
2 eggs, beaten

Cube the potatoes and cook thoroughly in salted water. Drain. Finely chop the onion, sauté in the olive oil until tender, and add to the potatoes. Season with salt and pepper. Coat the potato mixture lightly with the eggs.

Preheat the oven to 425 degrees.

Rub olive oil on a cookie sheet. Take one piece of the dough and stretch it out into a rectangle, about ¼ inch thick. Spread one third of the potato mixture over the dough and roll, pinching one end over the other to form a loaf, with minimal overlap. Repeat with the other two pieces.

Bake for about 25 minutes, or until lightly brown.

Universally acclaimed throughout the family—I can't think of one person who doesn't love this—is the ricotta calzone, called *cavazun* in the Roseto dialect. (We have no idea where this word comes from.) This is a sort of turnover, with a very flaky, light crust that remains white, stuffed with a sweetened ricotta filling. This is an excellent dessert, but like all the recipes in this chapter, it is perfect any time of the day.

Ricotta Calzone (Cavazun)
MAKES 4 TO 6

FILLING
6 eggs
1 cup sugar
2 teaspoons vanilla extract
2 pounds whole ricotta cheese, drained
1 teaspoon salt
¾ cup all-purpose flour
1 teaspoon baking powder

In a large bowl, beat the eggs and slowly add ½ cup of the sugar. Beat until light and pale gold in color. Add the vanilla.

In another large bowl, gently cream the ricotta with the salt, then slowly fold in the remaining ½ cup of sugar.

Fold the two mixtures together, and do not overmix. Then, in a separate bowl, combine the flour and baking powder. Fold into the first mixture. The resulting consistency should be slightly thicker than pancake batter. If it's too soft, add a little more flour. Chill for 30 minutes to 1 hour.

CRUST

2½ cups all-purpose flour
½ teaspoon salt
½ cup shortening
½ cup cold water

Mix the flour and salt in a bowl. Cut and add the shortening slowly, allowing the mixture to turn into crumbs. Add the water and form a ball that comes away clean from the sides of the bowl. Cover with plastic wrap and chill in the refrigerator.

GLAZE

1 egg yolk, beaten with 1 tablespoon water

Preheat the oven to 425 degrees.

Divide the dough into 10 small balls, about 3 to 4 inches in size. Generously flour a work surface. Use a rolling pin to roll each ball into a thin circle about 9 to 10 inches across.

Take about ¾ cup of the filling and place it in the center of the pastry. Fold the pastry in half. It should now look like a turnover. Crimp the edges all the way around and seal with a pastry cutter that has a serrated edge. (You can also seal the pastry with the tines of a fork.) Do not try to reuse any scraps of dough. Glaze the top of the closed pastry with the egg yolk mixture.

Transfer the pastry from the floured surface to a greased cookie sheet. You can use a spatula and your hand to help move it; it's a bit wet and heavy.

Bake for about 20 minutes, or until golden brown. Cool on a wire rack.

You knew you hit the mother lode if any one of these was in Grandmom Trigiani's bag on a road trip. Mary's favorite, though, by far, was the oil pretzel. She loved these so much that Grandmom would make them and ship them to her. On a car trip, they helped to pass the time and keep us full until the next meal.

The oil pretzel comes in two varieties: sweetened and unsweetened. Grand-

COOKING WITH MY SISTERS

mom tended to call them *biscotti*, but they're not what we know as biscotti today. These are excellent for babies, by the way, because they can chew on them during teething.

Grandmom's Oil Pretzels

MAKES 3 DOZEN

1 cup warm water
1 packet active dry yeast
1 cup sugar
12 eggs
1 cup vegetable oil
Pinch of salt
8 cups all-purpose flour

In a small bowl, combine the warm water and the yeast with 2 teaspoons of the sugar. Let the yeast rise—as long as it takes.

Using a mixer, combine the eggs and the remaining sugar. Then add the oil, salt, and some flour—not too much. Add the yeast mixture and more flour until a bread-like dough is formed.

When the beaters can't spin anymore, move the dough to a large cutting board and knead it. Use as much flour as it takes to make a soft dough; if it's sticky add a little more flour.

Put the dough back into the bowl, cover, and let stand for 20 to 30 minutes.

Preheat the oven to 375 degrees.

Turn the dough out of the bowl onto the cutting board. Pat it out to a rectangle about 1½ inches thick. Cut the dough into horizontal strips, about 2 inches wide, then cut them again vertically, at about 1-inch intervals. Important: Don't cut them too small or they will fall through the oven rack.

Put the pieces in boiling water for a few minutes, until they rise to the top. Remove and bake directly on the oven rack until they are brown on the bottom. Turn them over and let them brown on the other side.

Viola's Manhattan Cocktail

SERVES 1

2 ounces whiskey
1 ounce sweet vermouth
2 dashes Angostura bitters
A splash of maraschino cherry juice

Pour ingredients into a mixing glass with ice cubes; strain into a cocktail glass.
Serve straight-up and garnish with a maraschino cherry and orange peel twist.
      Pair with Oil Pretzels.

Many of these treats were prepared for holidays, too. When a holiday rolled around, only a feast would do. Advance preparation often took weeks.

Spring's arrival and the holiday of Easter were marked by the annual baking of *fuatha*, a traditional sweet bread that no doubt is a cousin to *panettone* and challah bread. Mary thinks that the dialect word *fuatha* may come from the verb *vuotare*, which means "to empty"—exactly what you do when you knead the dough, three times, to punch out all the air. Making the Easter bread, though, was a spectacular operation that yielded enough loaves to share with neighbors and to send to long-distance family. (As you see, this is a theme: Holidays mean connecting, and when we Trigianis reach out and touch someone, we do it with food.)

An old wives' tale says that fuatha dough will only rise in the spring, during Eastertide. I think it's true; we've tried to prepare it at other times of the year, but it just doesn't turn out as well. This is a blessing in disguise, because the process of making fuatha literally changed our lives for those few weeks in early spring. The dining room and the foyer—the sunniest, warmest rooms in our house—were overtaken with huge tubs of aromatic, fluffy dough. It would rise for hours, the sun coaxing the yeast to raise it, only to have Mom come through and pummel it so it would rise ever higher until it took two of us to carry the tubs into the kitchen, where she would pull strands of it, twist it into lush braids, and place it in the pans for baking.

✦ *Mom says:* "The first time I made fuatha by myself, it was a disaster. Even though I had watched Grandmom Trigiani make it, and recorded as much as I could in the way of ingredients, something went wrong. And Grandmom couldn't figure out what I did; she checked my recipe and it looked right. So I called her sister, Helen, to see what she thought. Aunt Helen came over to spend the day with me to take me through it step by step. I've never had a bad batch since!"

When the Easter bread was removed from the oven, puffy and warm, it was drenched in honey (Grandmom would sprinkle granulated sugar over the honey, which glistened like diamonds). We learned very early on that it was important for the food to be delicious, but beautiful as well. And this bread had many uses, whether to serve with coffee when visitors stopped by, as a late-night snack with hot chocolate, or toasted and buttered for breakfast.

Easter Bread (Fuatha)
MAKES 6 OR 7 RECTANGULAR LOAVES OR 4 ROUND LOAVES

1 tablespoon salt
7¼ pounds all-purpose flour, with 5 cups kept separate
3½ cups granulated sugar, with ½ cup set aside
2 packages active dry yeast
¾ cup lukewarm water (105–110 degrees)
2 cups warm milk (105–110 degrees)
4 oranges, for juice and zest (yields 1½ cups juice, ½ cup zest)
4 lemons, for juice and zest (yields 1½ cups juice, ½ cup zest)
½ pound (2 sticks) unsalted butter, cut into small pieces and softened
9 jumbo eggs (or 12 small or 10 medium eggs)
1½ tablespoons vanilla extract
1½ tablespoons lemon extract
1½ tablespoons orange extract
1½ ounces anisette
1½ ounces light rum

4 to 8 ounces vegetable shortening, for greasing pans
24 ounces honey, for brushing on finished loaves

In a large bowl, combine the salt, 5 cups of the flour, and 1 cup of the sugar. In a separate bowl, combine the yeast and the warm water. Dissolve the yeast and set aside for several minutes until bubbly. Then add the yeast mixture to the flour mixture. Add the 2 cups of warm milk to the mixture. Mix until you have a solid, sticky paste; cover with waxed paper and blankets and place in a warm room, preferably with sunlight. Allow to rise for approximately 3 hours, or until it is doubled in size.

Grate the zest from the oranges and lemons. Set the zest aside. Squeeze the juices from the oranges and lemons to equal 3 cups. Set aside.

In a mixer, beat the butter and 2 cups of the remaining sugar, adding the sugar gradually until the combination is light and fluffy. Add the eggs and beat until blended (do not overbeat!). Add the vanilla, lemon, and orange extracts, anisette, rum, lemon and orange zests, and lemon and orange juices.

Add this mixture to the rising dough. Mix together slowly and add the additional flour cup by cup—usually 4 to 5 pounds—until the dough becomes firm in consistency and satiny in texture. Knead very well.

Form the dough into one large round ball; butter the top thoroughly and cover with waxed paper and blankets. Place it in a warm room, preferably with sunlight. Allow the dough to double in size, approximately 4 to 5 hours. (We use a medium-size white plastic dishpan, reserved only for making Easter bread.)

When the dough has doubled in size, knead slightly and prepare loaves in one of three formats: rectangular loaf, round loaf, or round loaf of separate buns. All pans should be greased generously with vegetable shortening.

To make separate buns, take a piece of dough, about the size of a woman's fist, and roll it out between your hands to the proportion of a sausage. Place on a bread board and pat it down to about 2 inches in width and ½ inch in depth. Wrap the piece of dough around the first and middle fingers of your free hand, to about 3 inches in length. Tuck in the top end and place standing up in a round baking pan. Start by putting one bun in the middle and fill around the pan with buns also standing on end. Butter the tops and cover, allowing to rise until it's quite puffy, about 1 to 2 hours, and the dough doubles in size.

To make a round or rectangular loaf, place the dough directly in the pan. Butter the tops of the loaves and cover again. Allow the prepared loaves to rise for about 1 to 2 hours, until the dough doubles in size. When a round or rtangular loaf has risen fully, make shallow slashes in the tops in the form of a cross.

Preheat the oven to 275 degrees.

Bake until the tops are light brown and a toothpick, when inserted, comes out clean. Depending on the size of the loaves, this can take anywhere from 20 minutes to more than an hour.

When baked, remove from the oven and allow to cool for about an hour. Remove from pans while still warm, and allow to cool slightly on waxed paper; brush honey on top. When the bread is completely cool, brush with honey again, then wrap in waxed paper, then aluminum foil. (You have the option of sprinkling the extra ½ cup of sugar over the loaves after the second brushing with honey.)

NOTE: All ingredients should be at room temperature when preparation begins. The warmth of the house is instrumental in the times that are provided for the rising of the yeast mixture and dough. It is best to place the dough near a radiator or in a sunny spot so that the dough can enjoy the benefits of the warmest heat available. (Don't be afraid to push up the thermostat!) Also, cover the dough with waxed paper first so that in the event the dough touches the cloth, it can be easily removed. Finally, buttering the top of the dough before allowing it to rise prohibits a crusty top from forming, thus providing the best dough for kneading and ultimate result when baked.

Making the Easter bread with Mom, who learned it from Grandmom Trigiani and her sister, Aunt Helen, kept us connected to our traditions after our move to faraway Big Stone Gap. About Big Stone Gap, Grandmom said, "It's pretty, but I couldn't live in a place where they don't make cheese."

CHAPTER EIGHT

Things We Hated as Kids but Love to Serve Now

Toni, Mike, Checka, and Carlo hit the bricks.

*S*pezzad. Or as we liked to say, SPITzad. Little did we know that this was Roseto dialect for *spezzatino*, which means "stew" in Italian. And little did we know we would come to love it.

✦ *Checka says:* "Except for me."

Because when we were kids, we hated it, we dreaded it, and we ate as little of it as possible.

✦ *Checka says:* "Except Toni, who loved it. The rest of us would pick out the meat and eat only that."

Spezzad is a hearty stew that features greens, bites of veal or beef, Parmigiano-Reggiano cheese, and egg in a clear broth.

Ally and Anthony and Tiny Bubbles.

Spezzatino (Spezzad)

SERVES 10 TO 12

2 to 3 pounds veal, suitable for a stew
1 medium onion, finely chopped
½ cup olive oil
2 quarts chicken broth
2 large bunches of endive, any type
6 to 8 eggs
1 cup finely chopped Italian parsley
1 cup grated Parmigiano-Reggiano
Salt and freshly ground black pepper to taste

Using kitchen scissors, cut the veal into small pieces (smaller than bite-size).

In a large pot, brown the veal and onion in olive oil. Simmer until the meat is tender. Add the chicken broth. Set aside.

Steam the endive until tender. Chop fine. Add the endive to the soup stock. Bring this to a low boil.

Beat the eggs. Add the parsley and cheese, then season with salt and pepper. Drop the egg mixture into the boiling soup 15 minutes prior to serving.

Serve with Italian rolls or bread.

> *A Tip from Mom:* To save time, use frozen greens—even mustard greens are okay, as I discovered after moving to the South—but don't skip the steaming. And always do the chopping afterward because it helps to drain the maximum amount of water.

The thing was, adults love spezzad, especially guests at our house, who would welcome seconds. (We made it clear we thought they were simply pandering to Mom.) Of course, we pushed thirds on these unsuspecting victims, because the more that was eaten by company, the less there was for leftovers. If there was just a little, or not enough for the entire family, it was a good bet that Mom would save it for Dad's lunch on the weekend.

Even though Toni was the only one who liked the spezzad, Mom established, early on, that she was cooking one meal and one meal only, and we were going to learn to eat everything. This not only lessened the burden for her, it taught us an important lesson about being good guests.

When Mary was visiting the family in Bergamo, Mafalda liked to use the opportunity to prepare classic dishes, first because Don Andrea had excellent taste and liked a multicourse meal; second, because she loved to cook; and third, because she knew Mary liked to learn about the Italian way of dining. One time, Mafalda asked Mary if she'd like to try *vitello tonnato,* and like everyone else that hears this for the first time, Mary did a double take on the tuna "sauce." Fortified by Mom's training and her trust of Mafalda, Mary gave it a whirl. She now loves it. This truly unique dish is finally starting to show up on the menus of fine Italian restaurants in the larger American cities.

Mafalda's Vitello Tonnato (Veal with Tuna Sauce)

Prepare one day in advance

SERVES 6

2 cups chicken stock
1 onion, quartered
1 carrot, quartered
2 celery stalks, sliced
8 large but thin veal fillets
One 6½-ounce can imported Italian tuna, drained
4 anchovy fillets
⅔ cup olive oil
4 tablespoons capers, drained
3 tablespoons fresh lemon juice
1 cup mayonnaise
6 sprigs of Italian parsley

Combine the chicken stock, onion, carrot, and celery in a large skillet. Bring to a low boil. Add the veal, braising it very slowly. When the veal is cooked through, in just a few minutes, cover and remove the pan from the heat, leaving the veal in the pan. Refrigerate.

Using a blender or food processor, combine the tuna, anchovies, olive oil, 3 tablespoons of the capers, and the lemon juice. The sauce is ready when the texture is creamy and uniform.

In a large bowl, fold the sauce into the mayonnaise.

To prepare, spread a tablespoon or so of the sauce on a large platter. Place the pieces of veal side to side on the platter. Cover the veal with the remaining sauce and refrigerate for a day, covered with plastic wrap. To serve, bring the platter to room temperature. Garnish with the parsley and the remaining tablespoon of capers.

From tuna we move to anchovies. Now this is something most people avoid, unless they're going for a little flavor in a Caesar salad (note: A North American invention). But there is one dish that somehow reduces the negative impact of the anchovy to the point that most people, except children, really like it. Which means more for the grown-ups.

The dish is anchovy pizza, which is made like the potato pizza in the previous chapter. The best way to serve this is to cut it into half-inch slices. That way, the taste of the anchovies is not overwhelming and it balances nicely with the bread. However, if that's the way it's served, you *will* wind up eating a lot of it. I have never met anyone who doesn't love it.

Anchovy Pizza
MAKES 3 LOAVES

DOUGH
1 packet active dry yeast
1 cup warm water
2½ cups all-purpose flour
1 teaspoon salt
1 tablespoon olive oil

Dissolve the yeast in ¼ cup of the warm water and set aside until bubbly.

Combine the flour and the salt and mound on a cutting board, forming a well in the center. Add the yeast mixture, the remaining ¾ cup of water, and the olive oil and slowly draw in the flour. Keep mixing until all the flour has been added and continue to mix by hand. Knead until the dough is soft and elastic. Place in a bowl and rub with olive oil. Cover and let rise to about double the original size.

When the dough has risen, knead it again. Divide the dough into 3 even pieces.

FILLING
1 large sweet onion, finely chopped
¼ cup olive oil
2 cans anchovies packed in oil
Salt and freshly ground black pepper to taste

In a large skillet, cook the onion with the olive oil. Mix with the anchovies, being careful not to mush up the anchovies. Season with salt and pepper.

Preheat the oven to 425 degrees.

Rub olive oil on a cookie sheet. Take one piece of the dough and stretch it out into a rectangle, about ¼ inch thick. Spread one third of the anchovy mixture over the dough and roll, pinching one end over the other to form a loaf. Repeat with the other two pieces.

Bake for about 25 minutes, or until lightly brown.

To wind up the fish trio, we have Grandmom Trigiani's Cod Brodetto, a recipe I shared first in *Lucia, Lucia*. This soup is substantial, and it's terrific on pasta, which is how Grandmom served it. You can use regular cod fillets, but we recommend baccala, which is salt-cured cod.

Grandmom Trigiani's Cod Brodetto
SERVES 6

2 pounds salted cod fillets (baccala), cut into chunks
1 lemon
¼ cup olive oil
1 large sweet onion, sliced
3 garlic cloves, minced
6 fresh tomatoes, chopped
1 cup balsamic vinegar
2 quarts water
3 cups white wine
3 tablespoons chopped Italian parsley
Salt and freshly ground black pepper to taste

Place the cod on a large platter. Sprinkle it with the juice of the lemon and set aside.

In a large pot, heat the olive oil and lightly sauté the onion, garlic, tomatoes, and balsamic vinegar. Add the water and wine. Stir well. Add the seafood and parsley. Season with salt and pepper. Cook on the stovetop over medium heat for 40 minutes, or until the seafood cooks through. To serve, line soup bowls with thin slices of toasted Italian bread. Ladle the stew over the bread and serve.

We were not big fans of fish as kids, except maybe for fish sticks, because we got those on Friday nights if Dad wasn't home. Anyway, if Grandmom served the Cod Brodetto with a side of Dandelion Salad, and you didn't like the latter, you were sunk.

Dandelion Salad

Round up your grandchildren. Send them out into an open field to pull the green leaves from beneath the yellow flowers. Best to yank them before the tops turn to puffs. Tell the grandchildren to load them into a sack and run them to you in the kitchen.

Dandelion greens
8 tablespoons wine vinegar
2 tablespoons olive oil
1 teaspoon sugar
Pinch of salt

Separate the leaves by hand, wash, and throw into a bowl.

Whisk together the wine vinegar, olive oil, sugar, and salt. Toss over the leaves and serve.

Fortunately, if you didn't like dandelion greens, you were safe ninety percent of the year. Grandmom Trigiani never bought the greens, she just sent us out to forage, and there's a limited time they're available.

Cave people had nothing on us. Grandmom constantly had us on the side of the road grabbing stuff. If you were in the back of her car, and she saw a patch of something edible, you could bet that you'd be sent out to gather the berries, or whatever they were. (Grandmom made the best jam from wild raspberries.) Flowers were not exempt, either, unless, of course, they were in someone's yard.

During the summers in Pennsylvania, if you saw Trigiani grandchildren running along the side of the road, you knew Viola had them out collecting something. It was reminiscent of that scene in *The Sound of Music* in which the captain is driving home with the baroness (hiss) and sees all his children hanging from the big trees

lining the road. The only difference between us and the von Trapps is that they were having fun.

It was rare that we didn't like Grandmom's cookies, but her Fig and Date Cookies (*Fichi e Datteri Affettati*) were a taste we didn't acquire until adulthood. Probably because they are best with coffee. (I think of them as the Italian version of a breakfast bar, only better.) They can last for months if you store them in tins and put a layer of wax paper on top before sealing.

Fig and Date Cookies
MAKES 3 DOZEN

PASTRY
3 cups all-purpose flour
¾ cup sugar
½ teaspoon salt
¾ cup (1½ sticks) unsalted butter, softened
3 eggs
Pinch of grated lemon zest

FILLING
1 pound dried figs
1 cup dates
¼ cup boiling water
½ cup walnuts
3 ounces melted milk chocolate
1 tablespoon grated orange zest
2 tablespoons orange juice
4 tablespoons sugar
1 teaspoon cinnamon

On a work surface, mix the flour, sugar, and salt. Make a well in the center and add the butter, eggs, and lemon zest. Knead until sticky and refrigerate overnight.

Chop the figs and dates. Soak in the boiling water for 10 minutes. Remove the fruit from the water and grind it together with the walnuts. Add the rest of the filling ingredients and mix together. Cover and let stand for a few hours.

Preheat the oven to 375 degrees.

Roll out the dough into several rectangles. Line the center of each with filling. Wrap the sides of the dough over the top, pressing together gently. Turn upside-down and cut into pieces.

Bake until slightly brown, about 15 minutes. Let them cool off before packing.

If we turned our noses up at something on the table, there would be one of two common responses from our parents: "You people don't know what's good" (Dad) or "I want you to learn to eat everything" (Mom). Plus, there was the waste factor. This was an equal-opportunity obsession on both sides of our family. A person eats everything in front of him or her because it would be wrong to throw anything away, and not just because there are so many people without food in the world (although that was always part of the message, as it was in so many American homes). We learned that eating what was prepared for us was a sign of respect for the person who cooked it and the breadwinner who made it possible. To waste food was to waste goodwill. I can remember Grandmom Trigiani having special funnels for emptying the last drop of anything from a bottle or can, whether it was olive oil or ketchup. Everything was used. And reused. Viola never even threw away a jelly jar.

For Grandma Lucy, not wasting also meant sacrifice. When Grandpa Carlo died, times were tough. Mom remembers a knock at the door the Christmas after he died, and it was a man from one of Chisholm's civic clubs with a basket of fruit. He wanted to give it to Grandma Lucy, but she thanked him and refused. She said, "This is so kind of you, but I want you to give it to someone who needs it." While her kids never really wanted for anything, Mom said that basket would have come in handy. But Grandma Lucy couldn't even consider accepting something that she felt someone else needed more than she and her family did.

That was a defining lesson for Mom, her brother, and her sister. No surprise that the centerpiece of the story is food. In our family's corner of the world, food inspires and fuels, fascinates and sustains, tempts and teaches. It is a reason to come together, to remember, to learn, to create, to celebrate, to give. With luck, our *festa* will go on for a long, long time. And we'll leave the family treasure in even better shape than we found it.

Top: Ida's granddaughter Ella baking in Ida's kitchen. *Bottom:* Ida's grandson Luca preps food in Ida's kitchen.

Afterword

What I Learned on the Journey
Through Our Kitchen

Ida and her children in 2015 on the evening Ida was installed in the MECC Hall of Fame.
(Photo by Keith Dixon)

C hecka reminded me that Dad always used to say you should leave the world better than you found it. I had forgotten that I first heard this from him. They're extraordinarily powerful little words, *leave the world better than you found it*, and they can strengthen the resolve to do the right thing in the face of whatever challenges or irritates or even hurts. No family is perfect. And each one of the Trigianis would compete to be the first one to remind you of this fact, with an I-can-top-that story as proof. Siblings perfect the barb. Parents make mistakes. Grandparents pick favorites. Cousins poke fun. But in our expansive family, the positive messages are the most powerful, and these messages play out in an entertaining variety of ways. It's the reward I wouldn't trade for the perfect world of peace, quiet, and reason that once was my fantasy. Our family has helped me realize that just as there's affection in every cookie and a story in every strand of spaghetti, there is a laugh looking to be found in every conflict. Maybe it's because we're half Bergamaschi—as in the thespians who gave the world Punch, Judy, and the *commedia dell'arte*. Or perhaps it comes from being one quarter Veneziani—as in the adventurers who would just as soon throw you over the side of a gondola as they would serenade you. Or it could be from the part that is Pugliese—as in the mystics who invented superstition while they were directing traffic at the crossroads of every Mediterranean civilization. I like to think, though, that we find life's fun in the same way families all over the place do: by spending time together doing something we love. In our case, the connecting happens around the kitchen table. I hope that in this complicated world, every family can find a treasure to share passionately and graciously, and to laugh over, for the dear ones here now and those who surely will follow.

Mary Yolanda Trigiani, 2004

Epilogue

Make Your Meal Time Magical

Ida and her grandchildren.

One of the great gifts of meeting fellow authors after reading their books is observing the connection made between the writer and their creation, the substance of their work and their spiritual intent, and their ability to put their feelings out into the world and move readers with their insight, knowledge, and imagination.

When that author is also a chef, they have skills beyond writing the recipe. They follow their instructions and actually prepare delicious food, from a recipe of their own invention, that engages all five senses in preparation and presentation. They place their creation on the table, bringing their words to life, and it's personal.

How lucky I have been to meet some of the great chefs, but as we say, the bigger the star, the more humble he or she can be. Jacques Pepin prefers to be called a cook instead of a chef, even though his dishes are luscious and unforgettable, and have graced the tables of some of the fanciest places and people in the world.

Chef Pepin was humble and dignified, loved to laugh, and spoke of the preparation of food through the lens of his childhood, with stories about his mother and grandmother. It was then I realized that the art of cooking is the art of living, and we're all just, at our various levels (no one rivals Jacques!), savoring our childhood through the memory of how we felt when we enjoyed the traditional dishes that were prepared for us.

We imagine if we can remember the ingredients gathered in our grandmothers' gardens, carefully gleaned by them, observing them as they chose only the finest and freshest, instinctively measuring the components by sight, and finally cooked with largesse, we may bring back the best of what we came from, the nourishment that made us who we are. We are all, in cooking and baking family recipes, trying to get home, back to the kitchen, back to the place of warmth and belonging where we were fed good food and told stories that celebrated family history and lore.

Almost twenty years ago, when Viola Trigiani passed on, she had left her recipes buried behind her stove in a hiding place where only she could find them. When her oven died and had to be replaced, we found them, in her handwriting on bits of paper. Lucia Bonicelli's recipes had been written on index cards and filed by our mother, Ida, an organized librarian. Both of our grandmothers had their methods, but we are the beneficiaries of their good taste and generosity. And like Jacques Pepin, they considered themselves cooks, not chefs, but no matter the label, the results were divine.

Adriana Trigiani, 2017

See you in the kitchen! Ciao!

Index